50 Low-Carb Mexican Recipes for Home

By: Kelly Johnson

Table of Contents

Appetizers:

- Guacamole with Jicama or Cucumber Slices
- Ceviche with Shrimp or White Fish
- Mexican Stuffed Mini Peppers with Cream Cheese and Chorizo
- Zucchini Nachos with Ground Turkey
- Chicken or Beef Lettuce Wraps with Salsa Verde

Soups:

- Chicken Tortilla Soup (sans Tortillas)
- Spicy Mexican Cauliflower Soup
- Low-Carb Albondigas (Mexican Meatball Soup)
- Creamy Avocado Soup with Lime and Cilantro
- Chipotle Pumpkin Soup

Salads:

- Taco Salad with Ground Beef, Lettuce, Tomato, Avocado, and Cheese
- Mexican Cobb Salad with Grilled Chicken, Bacon, Avocado, and Queso Fresco
- Grilled Shrimp Salad with Avocado and Lime Dressing
- Cucumber and Tomato Salad with Cilantro and Lime
- Jicama and Mango Salad with Chili-Lime Dressing

Main Courses - Meat:

- Carne Asada with Grilled Vegetables
- Pork Carnitas Lettuce Wraps
- Beef Fajitas with Bell Peppers and Onions
- Chile Verde with Pork
- Mexican Shredded Chicken Tinga

Main Courses - Seafood:

- Fish Tacos in Lettuce Wraps with Cabbage Slaw

- Grilled Chipotle Lime Shrimp
- Baked Fish Veracruz Style
- Shrimp Enchiladas with Zucchini Tortillas
- Mahi Mahi with Avocado Salsa

Main Courses - Vegetarian:

- Portobello Mushroom Fajitas
- Cauliflower Rice Stuffed Peppers
- Vegetarian Enchiladas with Black Beans and Cheese
- Mexican Zucchini Boats with Ground Tofu
- Veggie Fajita Bowls with Guacamole and Sour Cream

Side Dishes:

- Mexican Cauliflower Rice
- Charred Mexican Street Corn (Elote) with Lime Crema
- Avocado and Tomato Salad with Cilantro Lime Vinaigrette
- Sautéed Garlic Spinach with Cotija Cheese
- Grilled Mexican Squash with Chili and Lime

Main Courses - Vegetarian:

- Mexican Cauliflower Rice
- Charred Mexican Street Corn (Elote) with Lime Crema
- Avocado and Tomato Salad with Cilantro Lime Vinaigrette
- Sautéed Garlic Spinach with Cotija Cheese
- Grilled Mexican Squash with Chili and Lime

Salsas and Sauces:

- Pico de Gallo
- Tomatillo Salsa Verde
- Roasted Red Pepper Salsa
- Chipotle Lime Crema
- Avocado Crema

Snacks:

- Spicy Mexican Roasted Nuts

- Queso Fundido with Chorizo and Bell Peppers (sans tortillas)
- Mexican Deviled Eggs with Guacamole
- Cheese Crisps with Jalapeño and Cilantro
- Mexican Stuffed Mushrooms with Cheese and Chorizo

Desserts:

- Mexican Chocolate Avocado Mousse
- Keto Tres Leches Cake
- Coconut Flan
- Sugar-Free Churros with Cinnamon and Stevia
- Mexican Spiced Dark Chocolate Truffles

Appetizers:

Guacamole with Jicama or Cucumber Slices

Ingredients:

- 2 ripe avocados
- 1 small red onion, finely diced
- 1-2 tomatoes, diced
- 1 jalapeño pepper, finely diced (seeds removed for less heat if desired)
- 1-2 cloves garlic, minced
- Juice of 1-2 limes
- Salt and pepper to taste
- Fresh cilantro leaves, chopped (optional)
- Jicama or cucumber, peeled and sliced for serving

Instructions:

Cut the avocados in half, remove the pits, and scoop the flesh into a mixing bowl.
Mash the avocado with a fork until it reaches your desired consistency (some prefer chunky, others prefer smooth).
Add the diced red onion, tomatoes, jalapeño pepper, and minced garlic to the mashed avocado.
Squeeze lime juice over the mixture and season with salt and pepper to taste.
Optionally, add chopped cilantro for extra flavor.
Gently fold all the ingredients together until well combined.
Taste the guacamole and adjust seasoning if necessary, adding more lime juice, salt, or pepper as desired.
Serve the guacamole with slices of jicama or cucumber on the side for dipping.

Enjoy this refreshing and low-carb twist on classic guacamole!

Ceviche with Shrimp or White Fish

Ingredients:

- 1 pound fresh shrimp or white fish fillets (such as tilapia, halibut, or sea bass), peeled and deveined (if using shrimp) or diced into small cubes (if using fish)
- 1 cup freshly squeezed lime juice (about 8-10 limes)
- 1 small red onion, thinly sliced
- 1-2 tomatoes, diced
- 1 jalapeño pepper, finely diced (seeds removed for less heat if desired)
- 1/2 cup chopped fresh cilantro
- 2-3 cloves garlic, minced
- Salt and pepper to taste
- Avocado slices, for garnish (optional)
- Tortilla chips or lettuce leaves, for serving

Instructions:

If using shrimp, bring a pot of salted water to a boil. Add the shrimp and cook for 1-2 minutes until they turn pink and opaque. Drain and rinse under cold water to stop the cooking process. Pat dry with paper towels. If using fish, ensure it's diced into small cubes.
In a glass or non-reactive bowl, combine the shrimp or fish with the freshly squeezed lime juice. Make sure the seafood is fully submerged in the lime juice. Cover the bowl with plastic wrap and refrigerate for at least 30 minutes to 1 hour, or until the shrimp or fish is "cooked" by the lime juice. The seafood should turn opaque and firm.
Once the seafood is "cooked," drain off most of the lime juice, leaving just a small amount to keep the ceviche moist.
Add the thinly sliced red onion, diced tomatoes, jalapeño pepper, chopped cilantro, and minced garlic to the bowl with the seafood. Mix gently to combine.
Season the ceviche with salt and pepper to taste.
Cover the ceviche and refrigerate for another 30 minutes to allow the flavors to meld together.
Before serving, taste the ceviche and adjust seasoning if necessary.
Serve the ceviche garnished with avocado slices, if desired, and accompanied by tortilla chips or lettuce leaves for scooping.

Enjoy this light and refreshing ceviche with shrimp or white fish, perfect for a low-carb appetizer or light meal!

Mexican Stuffed Mini Peppers with Cream Cheese and Chorizo

Ingredients:

- 12-15 mini sweet peppers, halved lengthwise and seeds removed
- 6 oz (170g) cream cheese, softened
- 1/2 cup cooked chorizo sausage, crumbled
- 1/2 cup shredded cheddar cheese
- 2 green onions, thinly sliced
- 1 teaspoon ground cumin
- 1/2 teaspoon chili powder
- Salt and pepper to taste
- Fresh cilantro leaves, for garnish (optional)

Instructions:

Preheat your oven to 375°F (190°C). Line a baking sheet with parchment paper or lightly grease it with cooking spray.

In a mixing bowl, combine the softened cream cheese, crumbled chorizo, shredded cheddar cheese, sliced green onions, ground cumin, and chili powder. Mix until well combined.

Season with salt and pepper to taste.

Spoon the cream cheese and chorizo mixture into the halved mini sweet peppers, filling each pepper half evenly.

Place the stuffed peppers on the prepared baking sheet, cut side up.

Bake in the preheated oven for 15-20 minutes, or until the peppers are tender and the filling is bubbly and lightly golden on top.

Once done, remove the stuffed peppers from the oven and let them cool slightly.

Garnish with fresh cilantro leaves, if desired, before serving.

Serve the Mexican stuffed mini peppers warm as a delicious appetizer or snack.

These stuffed peppers are packed with flavor and make a perfect low-carb addition to any

Mexican-inspired meal or party spread. Enjoy!

Zucchini Nachos with Ground Turkey

Ingredients:

- 2 medium zucchinis, sliced into thin rounds
- 1 tablespoon olive oil
- 1 pound ground turkey
- 1 packet taco seasoning (or homemade taco seasoning)
- 1 cup shredded cheddar cheese
- 1/2 cup diced tomatoes
- 1/4 cup diced red onion
- 1/4 cup sliced black olives
- 1/4 cup sliced jalapeños (optional)
- 1/4 cup chopped fresh cilantro
- Salt and pepper to taste
- Sour cream and guacamole for serving

Instructions:

Preheat your oven to 400°F (200°C). Line a baking sheet with parchment paper.
In a large skillet, heat the olive oil over medium heat. Add the ground turkey and cook, breaking it apart with a spoon, until it's browned and cooked through.
Stir in the taco seasoning and cook for another 2-3 minutes, until the turkey is evenly coated. Remove from heat and set aside.
Arrange the zucchini rounds in a single layer on the prepared baking sheet. Season with salt and pepper.
Spread the cooked ground turkey evenly over the zucchini rounds.
Sprinkle shredded cheddar cheese over the ground turkey and zucchini.
Top with diced tomatoes, diced red onion, sliced black olives, and sliced jalapeños (if using).
Bake in the preheated oven for 10-12 minutes, or until the cheese is melted and bubbly.
Remove from the oven and sprinkle chopped fresh cilantro over the top.
Serve the zucchini nachos hot, garnished with sour cream and guacamole on the side.

Enjoy these zucchini nachos with ground turkey as a delicious and low-carb twist on traditional nachos!

Chicken or Beef Lettuce Wraps with Salsa Verde

Ingredients:

For the Filling:

- 1 pound ground chicken or beef
- 1 tablespoon olive oil
- 1 small onion, finely diced
- 2 cloves garlic, minced
- 1 teaspoon ground cumin
- 1 teaspoon chili powder
- Salt and pepper to taste
- 1/2 cup salsa verde (store-bought or homemade)
- 1/4 cup chopped fresh cilantro
- Juice of 1 lime

For the Lettuce Wraps:

- Large lettuce leaves (such as iceberg or butter lettuce)
- Optional toppings: diced tomatoes, diced avocado, shredded cheese, sour cream

Instructions:

Heat olive oil in a large skillet over medium heat. Add the diced onion and cook until softened, about 2-3 minutes.

Add the minced garlic and cook for another minute until fragrant.

Add the ground chicken or beef to the skillet, breaking it apart with a spoon. Cook until browned and cooked through.

Stir in the ground cumin, chili powder, salt, and pepper. Cook for another minute to allow the spices to toast and become fragrant.

Add the salsa verde to the skillet and stir to combine with the meat. Let it simmer for a few minutes to allow the flavors to meld together.

Remove the skillet from heat and stir in the chopped cilantro and lime juice.

To assemble the lettuce wraps, spoon some of the chicken or beef filling onto each lettuce leaf.

Add optional toppings such as diced tomatoes, diced avocado, shredded cheese, and sour cream as desired.
Serve immediately and enjoy these delicious chicken or beef lettuce wraps with salsa verde!

These lettuce wraps are not only low-carb but also packed with flavor and perfect for a quick and healthy meal.

Soups:

Chicken Tortilla Soup (sans Tortillas)

Ingredients:

- 1 tablespoon olive oil
- 1 onion, diced
- 2 cloves garlic, minced
- 1 jalapeño, seeded and diced
- 1 red bell pepper, diced
- 1 teaspoon ground cumin
- 1 teaspoon chili powder
- 1/2 teaspoon paprika
- 4 cups chicken broth
- 1 (14.5 oz) can diced tomatoes
- 1 cup shredded cooked chicken breast
- 1 cup frozen corn kernels
- 1 (15 oz) can black beans, drained and rinsed
- Juice of 1 lime
- Salt and pepper to taste
- Avocado slices, chopped cilantro, lime wedges, and sour cream for serving

Instructions:

In a large pot or Dutch oven, heat the olive oil over medium heat. Add the diced onion, minced garlic, and diced jalapeño. Cook for about 5 minutes, or until the vegetables are softened.
Add the diced red bell pepper to the pot and cook for another 3-4 minutes.
Stir in the ground cumin, chili powder, and paprika. Cook for 1 minute, stirring constantly, until fragrant.
Pour in the chicken broth and diced tomatoes with their juices. Bring the soup to a simmer.
Add the shredded cooked chicken breast, frozen corn kernels, and black beans to the pot. Let the soup simmer for about 15-20 minutes to allow the flavors to meld together.
Stir in the lime juice and season the soup with salt and pepper to taste.

Ladle the soup into bowls and serve with avocado slices, chopped cilantro, lime wedges, and sour cream on top.
Enjoy this delicious and comforting chicken tortilla soup without the tortillas!

This soup is packed with flavor and hearty ingredients, making it a satisfying meal on its own or paired with a side salad for a complete low-carb dinner.

Spicy Mexican Cauliflower Soup

Ingredients:

- 1 tablespoon olive oil
- 1 onion, chopped
- 3 cloves garlic, minced
- 1 jalapeño, seeded and chopped
- 1 teaspoon ground cumin
- 1/2 teaspoon chili powder
- 1/2 teaspoon smoked paprika
- 1 large head cauliflower, chopped into florets
- 4 cups vegetable or chicken broth
- 1 (14.5 oz) can diced tomatoes
- Salt and pepper to taste
- Juice of 1 lime
- Optional toppings: chopped cilantro, avocado slices, sour cream, shredded cheese, tortilla strips

Instructions:

Heat the olive oil in a large pot over medium heat. Add the chopped onion and cook until softened, about 5 minutes.

Add the minced garlic and chopped jalapeño to the pot. Cook for another 2-3 minutes, until fragrant.

Stir in the ground cumin, chili powder, and smoked paprika. Cook for 1 minute, stirring constantly.

Add the chopped cauliflower florets to the pot, along with the vegetable or chicken broth and diced tomatoes. Bring the soup to a simmer.

Reduce the heat to low, cover the pot, and let the soup simmer for about 20-25 minutes, or until the cauliflower is tender.

Use an immersion blender to puree the soup until smooth. Alternatively, you can carefully transfer the soup in batches to a blender and blend until smooth, then return it to the pot.

Season the soup with salt, pepper, and lime juice to taste. Adjust the seasoning as needed.

Ladle the soup into bowls and serve hot, garnished with chopped cilantro, avocado slices, sour cream, shredded cheese, or tortilla strips if desired.

Enjoy this spicy Mexican cauliflower soup as a flavorful and satisfying low-carb meal!

This soup is packed with Mexican-inspired flavors and the cauliflower adds a creamy texture without the need for high-carb thickeners. It's perfect for a cozy night in or for serving at gatherings with friends and family.

Low-Carb Albondigas (Mexican Meatball Soup)

Ingredients:

For the Meatballs:

- 1 pound ground beef (or a mixture of beef and pork)
- 1/4 cup almond flour
- 1/4 cup grated Parmesan cheese
- 1 egg
- 2 cloves garlic, minced
- 1 teaspoon ground cumin
- 1 teaspoon dried oregano
- Salt and pepper to taste

For the Soup:

- 1 tablespoon olive oil
- 1 onion, diced
- 2 carrots, diced
- 2 stalks celery, diced
- 4 cups beef or chicken broth
- 1 (14.5 oz) can diced tomatoes
- 2 cups chopped spinach or kale
- Salt and pepper to taste
- Fresh cilantro, chopped, for garnish
- Lime wedges, for serving

Instructions:

In a large mixing bowl, combine all the ingredients for the meatballs: ground beef, almond flour, Parmesan cheese, egg, minced garlic, ground cumin, dried oregano, salt, and pepper. Mix until well combined.
Shape the meat mixture into small meatballs, about 1 inch in diameter.
Heat olive oil in a large pot over medium heat. Add the diced onion, carrots, and celery. Cook for about 5 minutes, or until the vegetables are softened.
Pour the broth into the pot and bring to a simmer.
Carefully add the meatballs to the simmering broth. Let the meatballs cook for about 10-15 minutes, or until cooked through.

Once the meatballs are cooked, add the diced tomatoes and chopped spinach or kale to the pot. Let the soup simmer for another 5-10 minutes, until the greens are wilted and the flavors are well combined.
Taste the soup and season with salt and pepper as needed.
Ladle the soup into bowls and garnish with chopped cilantro.
Serve hot with lime wedges on the side for squeezing over the soup.

Enjoy this delicious and comforting Low-Carb Albondigas soup, packed with flavorful meatballs and nutritious vegetables!

Creamy Avocado Soup with Lime and Cilantro

Ingredients:

- 2 ripe avocados
- 2 cups vegetable or chicken broth
- 1/2 cup Greek yogurt or sour cream
- Juice of 2 limes
- 1/4 cup chopped fresh cilantro leaves
- Salt and pepper to taste
- Optional toppings: diced tomatoes, chopped cilantro, sliced green onions, crumbled feta cheese, diced avocado, tortilla strips

Instructions:

Prepare the avocados: Cut the avocados in half and remove the pits. Scoop out the flesh and place it in a blender or food processor.

Blend the ingredients: Add the vegetable or chicken broth, Greek yogurt or sour cream, lime juice, and chopped cilantro to the blender with the avocado. Blend until smooth and creamy.

Season the soup: Taste the soup and season with salt and pepper to your liking. Blend again briefly to incorporate the seasoning.

Chill the soup: Transfer the soup to a bowl and cover it. Place it in the refrigerator to chill for at least 30 minutes, or until ready to serve.

Serve: Ladle the chilled avocado soup into bowls. Garnish with your choice of toppings, such as diced tomatoes, chopped cilantro, sliced green onions, crumbled feta cheese, diced avocado, or tortilla strips.

Enjoy: Serve the creamy avocado soup with lime and cilantro cold, and enjoy its refreshing flavors!

This soup is not only delicious but also packed with healthy fats from the avocado and a burst of citrusy freshness from the lime and cilantro. It's perfect as a starter for a summer meal or as a light lunch on its own.

Chipotle Pumpkin Soup

Ingredients:

- 2 tablespoons olive oil
- 1 onion, diced
- 3 cloves garlic, minced
- 1 chipotle pepper in adobo sauce, minced (adjust to taste)
- 1 teaspoon ground cumin
- 1/2 teaspoon ground cinnamon
- 1/4 teaspoon ground nutmeg
- 1 can (15 ounces) pumpkin puree
- 4 cups vegetable broth
- 1 cup coconut milk
- Salt and pepper to taste
- Optional toppings: toasted pumpkin seeds, chopped fresh cilantro, sour cream or Greek yogurt, lime wedges

Instructions:

Sauté aromatics: In a large pot, heat the olive oil over medium heat. Add the diced onion and cook until softened, about 5 minutes. Add the minced garlic and chipotle pepper and cook for another 1-2 minutes, until fragrant.

Add spices: Stir in the ground cumin, ground cinnamon, and ground nutmeg. Cook for an additional minute to toast the spices and enhance their flavor.

Combine pumpkin and broth: Add the pumpkin puree and vegetable broth to the pot. Stir well to combine all the ingredients.

Simmer: Bring the soup to a simmer over medium heat. Allow it to cook for about 15-20 minutes, stirring occasionally, to allow the flavors to meld together.

Blend the soup: Using an immersion blender or transferring the soup in batches to a blender, carefully blend the soup until smooth and creamy.

Add coconut milk: Stir in the coconut milk until well combined. Taste the soup and season with salt and pepper as needed.

Serve: Ladle the chipotle pumpkin soup into bowls. Garnish with your choice of toppings, such as toasted pumpkin seeds, chopped fresh cilantro, a dollop of sour cream or Greek yogurt, and a squeeze of fresh lime juice.

Enjoy: Serve the soup warm and enjoy its comforting flavors with a touch of smokiness from the chipotle pepper.

This Chipotle Pumpkin Soup is perfect for chilly autumn days or whenever you're craving a cozy and flavorful meal. It's vegan-friendly, gluten-free, and packed with nutritious ingredients, making it a great addition to your menu rotation.

Salads:

Taco Salad with Ground Beef, Lettuce, Tomato, Avocado, and Cheese

Ingredients:

- 1 pound ground beef
- 1 packet taco seasoning mix (or homemade taco seasoning)
- 1 head of lettuce (romaine or iceberg), chopped
- 2 tomatoes, diced
- 1 avocado, diced
- 1 cup shredded cheddar cheese
- 1/2 cup diced red onion (optional)
- 1/2 cup sliced black olives (optional)
- Tortilla chips or strips, for serving
- Your favorite salsa and/or dressing, for serving

Instructions:

Cook the ground beef: In a skillet over medium heat, cook the ground beef until browned and cooked through, breaking it up into crumbles as it cooks. Drain any excess fat. Add the taco seasoning mix and water according to the package instructions. Stir well to combine, then simmer for a few minutes until the flavors meld together. Remove from heat and set aside.
Prepare the salad base: In a large bowl, combine the chopped lettuce, diced tomatoes, diced avocado, shredded cheddar cheese, diced red onion (if using), and sliced black olives (if using). Toss gently to combine.
Assemble the salad: Add the cooked ground beef on top of the salad mixture.
Serve: Serve the taco salad immediately, with tortilla chips or strips on the side for added crunch. Offer your favorite salsa and/or dressing for drizzling over the salad.
Enjoy: Enjoy your delicious Taco Salad with Ground Beef, Lettuce, Tomato, Avocado, and Cheese!

Feel free to customize this taco salad recipe according to your preferences. You can add other toppings such as sliced jalapeños, diced bell peppers, corn kernels, or black beans. Additionally, you can use a different type of cheese or experiment with different dressings to suit your taste.

Mexican Cobb Salad with Grilled Chicken, Bacon, Avocado, and Queso Fresco

Ingredients:

- 2 boneless, skinless chicken breasts
- Salt and pepper to taste
- 6 slices bacon
- 6 cups mixed salad greens (romaine, spinach, arugula, etc.)
- 2 ripe avocados, diced
- 1 cup cherry tomatoes, halved
- 1/2 cup crumbled queso fresco
- 1/4 cup chopped fresh cilantro
- 2 hard-boiled eggs, sliced
- 1/4 cup sliced green onions
- Lime wedges, for serving

Dressing:

- 1/4 cup olive oil
- 2 tablespoons lime juice
- 1 clove garlic, minced
- 1 teaspoon honey or agave syrup
- 1/2 teaspoon ground cumin
- Salt and pepper to taste

Instructions:

Grill the chicken: Season the chicken breasts with salt and pepper. Preheat a grill or grill pan over medium-high heat. Grill the chicken for 6-8 minutes per side, or until cooked through and no longer pink in the center. Remove from the grill and let it rest for a few minutes before slicing.

Cook the bacon: In a skillet over medium heat, cook the bacon until crispy. Transfer to a paper towel-lined plate to drain excess grease. Once cooled, chop the bacon into bite-sized pieces.

Prepare the dressing: In a small bowl, whisk together the olive oil, lime juice, minced garlic, honey or agave syrup, ground cumin, salt, and pepper until well combined. Set aside.

Assemble the salad: In a large serving bowl or platter, arrange the mixed salad greens. Top with sliced grilled chicken, diced avocado, halved cherry tomatoes,

crumbled queso fresco, chopped bacon, sliced hard-boiled eggs, and sliced green onions. Sprinkle chopped fresh cilantro over the salad.
Serve: Drizzle the dressing over the salad just before serving. Serve the Mexican Cobb Salad with lime wedges on the side for an extra burst of flavor.
Enjoy: Serve immediately and enjoy this delicious and satisfying Mexican Cobb Salad with Grilled Chicken, Bacon, Avocado, and Queso Fresco!

Feel free to customize this salad by adding other ingredients such as black beans, corn kernels, roasted red peppers, or jalapeño slices. You can also adjust the dressing according to your taste preferences, adding more lime juice for acidity or honey for sweetness.

Grilled Shrimp Salad with Avocado and Lime Dressing

Ingredients:

For the Grilled Shrimp:

- 1 pound large shrimp, peeled and deveined
- 2 tablespoons olive oil
- 2 cloves garlic, minced
- 1 teaspoon paprika
- 1/2 teaspoon cumin
- Salt and pepper to taste

For the Salad:

- 6 cups mixed salad greens (such as lettuce, spinach, arugula)
- 1 avocado, diced
- 1 cup cherry tomatoes, halved
- 1/4 cup thinly sliced red onion
- 1/4 cup chopped fresh cilantro
- Optional: sliced jalapeños for heat

For the Lime Dressing:

- 1 ripe avocado
- Juice of 2 limes
- 1/4 cup olive oil
- 2 tablespoons chopped fresh cilantro
- 1 clove garlic, minced
- Salt and pepper to taste

Instructions:

For the Grilled Shrimp:

In a bowl, combine olive oil, minced garlic, paprika, cumin, salt, and pepper. Add the shrimp to the bowl and toss until evenly coated.
Preheat grill to medium-high heat. Thread shrimp onto skewers or use a grill basket to prevent them from falling through the grates.
Grill shrimp for 2-3 minutes per side, or until they are pink and opaque. Remove from heat and set aside.

For the Lime Dressing:

In a blender or food processor, combine the flesh of one ripe avocado, lime juice, olive oil, chopped cilantro, minced garlic, salt, and pepper. Blend until smooth and creamy. If the dressing is too thick, you can add a little water to thin it out.
Taste and adjust seasoning as needed. Set aside.

Assembling the Salad:

In a large bowl, combine the mixed salad greens, diced avocado, halved cherry tomatoes, thinly sliced red onion, and chopped cilantro. Toss gently to combine.
Divide the salad among plates or bowls. Top each salad with grilled shrimp and optional sliced jalapeños.
Drizzle the avocado lime dressing over the salads just before serving.
Garnish with additional chopped cilantro, if desired.
Serve immediately and enjoy your Grilled Shrimp Salad with Avocado and Lime Dressing!

This salad is bursting with flavor from the grilled shrimp, creamy avocado, and zesty lime dressing. It's perfect for a light lunch or dinner, and you can customize it with your favorite toppings or additional protein sources like grilled chicken or tofu.

Cucumber and Tomato Salad with Cilantro and Lime

Ingredients:

- 2 large cucumbers, thinly sliced
- 2 large tomatoes, diced
- 1/4 cup chopped fresh cilantro leaves
- Juice of 1-2 limes (depending on preference)
- 2 tablespoons extra virgin olive oil
- Salt and pepper to taste
- Optional: red onion, thinly sliced for added flavor and color

Instructions:

In a large bowl, combine the thinly sliced cucumbers, diced tomatoes, and chopped cilantro.
In a small bowl, whisk together the lime juice and extra virgin olive oil to make the dressing. Season with salt and pepper to taste.
Pour the dressing over the cucumber and tomato mixture. Toss gently to coat all the ingredients evenly with the dressing.
Taste and adjust seasoning as needed, adding more salt, pepper, or lime juice if desired.
Optional: Add thinly sliced red onion to the salad for added flavor and color.
Serve the Cucumber and Tomato Salad with Cilantro and Lime immediately, or refrigerate for 30 minutes to allow the flavors to meld together before serving.
Enjoy your refreshing and flavorful salad as a side dish or light lunch option!

This salad is perfect for summer picnics, barbecues, or as a quick and healthy side dish any time of the year. The combination of fresh cucumbers, juicy tomatoes, zesty lime, and fragrant cilantro creates a deliciously vibrant salad that's sure to be a hit with family and friends.

Jicama and Mango Salad with Chili-Lime Dressing

Ingredients:

For the Salad:

- 1 medium jicama, peeled and julienned
- 2 ripe mangoes, peeled and julienned
- 1/4 cup chopped fresh cilantro
- 1/4 cup chopped fresh mint leaves
- 1/4 cup chopped red onion
- Optional: 1/4 cup chopped roasted peanuts or pepitas for added crunch

For the Chili-Lime Dressing:

- Juice of 2-3 limes
- 2 tablespoons honey or agave syrup
- 1 tablespoon olive oil
- 1 teaspoon chili powder (adjust to taste)
- 1/2 teaspoon ground cumin
- Salt to taste

Instructions:

In a large bowl, combine the julienned jicama, julienned mangoes, chopped cilantro, chopped mint leaves, and chopped red onion. Toss gently to mix all the ingredients.

In a small bowl, whisk together the lime juice, honey or agave syrup, olive oil, chili powder, ground cumin, and salt to make the dressing. Adjust the sweetness and spiciness according to your taste preferences.

Pour the chili-lime dressing over the jicama and mango mixture. Toss gently to coat all the ingredients evenly with the dressing.

Optional: Sprinkle chopped roasted peanuts or pepitas over the salad for added crunch and flavor.

Serve the Jicama and Mango Salad with Chili-Lime Dressing immediately, or refrigerate for 30 minutes to allow the flavors to meld together before serving.

Enjoy your refreshing and flavorful salad as a side dish or light meal!

This Jicama and Mango Salad with Chili-Lime Dressing is perfect for summer gatherings, potlucks, or as a refreshing side dish to complement grilled meats or seafood. The combination of crunchy jicama, sweet mangoes, fragrant herbs, and zesty dressing creates a tantalizing flavor experience that's sure to impress your family and friends.

Main Courses - Meat:

Carne Asada with Grilled Vegetables

Ingredients:

For the Carne Asada:

- 2 pounds flank steak or skirt steak
- Juice of 2-3 limes
- 4 cloves garlic, minced
- 1/4 cup chopped fresh cilantro
- 2 tablespoons olive oil
- 1 teaspoon ground cumin
- 1 teaspoon chili powder
- Salt and pepper to taste

For the Grilled Vegetables:

- Assorted vegetables, such as bell peppers, zucchini, yellow squash, red onion, and mushrooms, sliced
- 2 tablespoons olive oil
- Salt and pepper to taste
- Optional: additional seasonings like garlic powder, onion powder, or Italian seasoning

For Serving:

- Corn or flour tortillas
- Salsa, guacamole, sour cream, or your favorite toppings

Instructions:

For the Carne Asada:

In a bowl, combine the lime juice, minced garlic, chopped cilantro, olive oil, ground cumin, chili powder, salt, and pepper to make the marinade.

Place the flank steak or skirt steak in a shallow dish or resealable plastic bag. Pour the marinade over the steak, making sure it's well coated. Cover or seal and refrigerate for at least 2 hours, or preferably overnight, to allow the flavors to penetrate the meat.

Preheat your grill to medium-high heat. Remove the steak from the marinade and discard any excess marinade.

Grill the steak for 4-6 minutes per side, or until it reaches your desired level of doneness. Flank steak and skirt steak are best when cooked to medium-rare or medium. Remove the steak from the grill and let it rest for a few minutes before slicing thinly against the grain.

For the Grilled Vegetables:

In a large bowl, toss the sliced vegetables with olive oil, salt, pepper, and any additional seasonings of your choice until evenly coated.
Preheat your grill to medium-high heat. Place the seasoned vegetables on the grill grates in a single layer or use a grill basket to prevent them from falling through.
Grill the vegetables for 5-7 minutes, turning occasionally, or until they are tender and lightly charred.

For Serving:

Slice the grilled carne asada thinly against the grain.
Serve the carne asada and grilled vegetables with warm tortillas and your favorite toppings such as salsa, guacamole, sour cream, or chopped cilantro.
Enjoy your delicious Carne Asada with Grilled Vegetables!

This dish is perfect for a festive outdoor meal with family and friends. The tender and flavorful carne asada pairs beautifully with the smoky grilled vegetables, creating a satisfying and memorable dining experience.

Pork Carnitas Lettuce Wraps

Ingredients:

For the Pork Carnitas:

- 2 pounds pork shoulder or pork butt, cut into chunks
- 1 onion, roughly chopped
- 4 cloves garlic, minced
- 1 teaspoon ground cumin
- 1 teaspoon dried oregano
- 1 teaspoon smoked paprika
- 1 teaspoon chili powder
- 1/2 teaspoon ground coriander
- 1/2 teaspoon ground cinnamon
- 1/2 teaspoon salt
- Juice of 2 oranges
- Juice of 1 lime
- 1/4 cup chopped fresh cilantro
- 2 tablespoons olive oil
- 1 cup chicken or beef broth

For Serving:

- Large lettuce leaves (such as romaine or butter lettuce)
- Sliced avocado
- Chopped fresh cilantro
- Diced red onion
- Lime wedges

Instructions:

For the Pork Carnitas:

> In a large bowl, combine the pork chunks, chopped onion, minced garlic, ground cumin, dried oregano, smoked paprika, chili powder, ground coriander, ground cinnamon, and salt.
> Add the juice of the oranges and lime, chopped cilantro, and olive oil to the bowl. Toss the pork mixture until evenly coated with the marinade. Cover the bowl and refrigerate for at least 2 hours, or preferably overnight, to allow the flavors to meld.
> Preheat your oven to 325°F (160°C).

Transfer the marinated pork mixture to a Dutch oven or large oven-safe pot. Add the chicken or beef broth to the pot, ensuring that the pork is mostly submerged in liquid. Cover the pot with a lid and transfer it to the preheated oven. Cook the pork carnitas for 2.5 to 3 hours, or until the meat is tender and easily shreds with a fork.
Once the pork is cooked, remove the pot from the oven and use two forks to shred the meat into bite-sized pieces. Return the shredded pork to the pot and toss it in the cooking juices to coat.

For Serving:

Wash and dry the lettuce leaves, then arrange them on a serving platter.
Spoon the cooked pork carnitas onto the lettuce leaves, dividing evenly among them.
Top the pork carnitas with sliced avocado, chopped cilantro, diced red onion, and a squeeze of lime juice.
Serve the Pork Carnitas Lettuce Wraps immediately, allowing diners to assemble their own wraps according to their preferences.
Enjoy your flavorful and satisfying Pork Carnitas Lettuce Wraps!

These lettuce wraps are not only delicious and satisfying but also low in carbs, making them a great option for those following a low-carb or keto diet. The tender and flavorful pork carnitas pair beautifully with the crisp and fresh lettuce leaves, creating a delightful contrast of textures and flavors.

Beef Fajitas with Bell Peppers and Onions

Ingredients:

For the Marinade:

- 1/4 cup olive oil
- Juice of 2 limes
- 4 cloves garlic, minced
- 1 teaspoon chili powder
- 1 teaspoon ground cumin
- 1 teaspoon smoked paprika
- 1/2 teaspoon dried oregano
- Salt and pepper to taste

For the Beef Fajitas:

- 1.5 pounds flank steak or skirt steak, sliced thinly against the grain
- 2 bell peppers (any color), sliced
- 1 large onion, sliced
- 2 tablespoons vegetable oil or canola oil
- Salt and pepper to taste
- Flour or corn tortillas, for serving
- Optional toppings: salsa, guacamole, sour cream, shredded cheese, chopped cilantro, lime wedges

Instructions:

For the Marinade:

In a bowl, whisk together the olive oil, lime juice, minced garlic, chili powder, ground cumin, smoked paprika, dried oregano, salt, and pepper to make the marinade.
Place the sliced beef in a shallow dish or resealable plastic bag. Pour the marinade over the beef, making sure it's well coated. Cover or seal and refrigerate for at least 30 minutes, or up to 4 hours, to allow the flavors to penetrate the meat.

For the Beef Fajitas:

Heat 1 tablespoon of vegetable oil in a large skillet or cast-iron pan over medium-high heat.
Add the sliced bell peppers and onions to the skillet. Season with salt and pepper to taste. Cook, stirring occasionally, for 5-7 minutes, or until the vegetables are tender and slightly caramelized. Remove the cooked vegetables from the skillet and set aside.

In the same skillet, add the remaining tablespoon of vegetable oil. Remove the marinated beef from the marinade and shake off any excess.

Add the sliced beef to the skillet in a single layer, making sure not to overcrowd the pan. Cook the beef for 2-3 minutes per side, or until browned and cooked to your desired level of doneness. Cook the beef in batches if necessary to avoid overcrowding the pan.

Once the beef is cooked, return the cooked vegetables to the skillet. Toss everything together to combine and heat through.

Warm the tortillas in a dry skillet or microwave according to package instructions.

Serve the Beef Fajitas with Bell Peppers and Onions with warm tortillas and your choice of toppings such as salsa, guacamole, sour cream, shredded cheese, chopped cilantro, and lime wedges.

Enjoy your delicious Beef Fajitas with Bell Peppers and Onions!

These beef fajitas are perfect for a quick and satisfying weeknight meal or for entertaining guests. The tender and flavorful beef, paired with the colorful bell peppers and onions, creates a delicious and satisfying dish that's sure to be a hit with your family and friends.

Chile Verde with Pork

Ingredients:

For the Chile Verde:

- 2 pounds pork shoulder or pork butt, trimmed of excess fat and cut into bite-sized pieces
- 2 tablespoons vegetable oil
- 1 onion, chopped
- 4 cloves garlic, minced
- 2 cans (4 ounces each) diced green chilies
- 2 jalapeño peppers, seeded and chopped (optional, for added heat)
- 1 cup chicken broth or water
- 1 teaspoon ground cumin
- 1 teaspoon dried oregano
- Salt and pepper to taste
- Chopped fresh cilantro for garnish

For Serving:

- Cooked rice
- Warm tortillas
- Lime wedges
- Chopped fresh cilantro
- Sliced radishes
- Sour cream or Mexican crema
- Sliced avocado

Instructions:

Heat the vegetable oil in a large pot or Dutch oven over medium-high heat. Add the chopped onion and cook until softened, about 5 minutes.

Add the minced garlic and cook for an additional minute, until fragrant.

Add the bite-sized pieces of pork to the pot, season with salt and pepper, and cook until browned on all sides.

Stir in the diced green chilies, chopped jalapeño peppers (if using), ground cumin, and dried oregano. Cook for another minute to toast the spices.

Pour in the chicken broth or water, scraping up any browned bits from the bottom of the pot for added flavor.

Bring the mixture to a simmer, then reduce the heat to low. Cover the pot and let the Chile Verde simmer gently for 1.5 to 2 hours, or until the pork is tender and the flavors have melded together.
Taste and adjust the seasoning with salt and pepper as needed.
Once the pork is tender and the sauce has thickened slightly, remove the pot from the heat.
Serve the Chile Verde with cooked rice and warm tortillas. Garnish with chopped fresh cilantro, sliced radishes, a squeeze of lime juice, and a dollop of sour cream or Mexican crema.
Enjoy your delicious Chile Verde with Pork!

This Chile Verde with Pork is hearty, flavorful, and perfect for serving as a main course for a family dinner or gathering with friends. The tender pork and savory green chili sauce pair wonderfully with rice, tortillas, and a variety of toppings for a satisfying and delicious meal.

Mexican Shredded Chicken Tinga

Ingredients:

For the Chicken Tinga:

- 2 pounds boneless, skinless chicken breasts or thighs
- 1 onion, chopped
- 3 cloves garlic, minced
- 2 chipotle peppers in adobo sauce, chopped
- 1 can (14.5 ounces) diced tomatoes
- 1 teaspoon dried oregano
- 1 teaspoon ground cumin
- 1/2 teaspoon smoked paprika
- 1/2 teaspoon chili powder
- Salt and pepper to taste
- 1 tablespoon vegetable oil

For Serving:

- Corn or flour tortillas
- Chopped fresh cilantro
- Diced onion
- Crumbled queso fresco or shredded Monterey Jack cheese
- Sliced avocado
- Lime wedges

Instructions:

In a large skillet or Dutch oven, heat the vegetable oil over medium heat. Add the chopped onion and cook until softened, about 5 minutes.

Add the minced garlic to the skillet and cook for another minute, until fragrant.

Season the chicken breasts or thighs with salt and pepper, then add them to the skillet. Cook until browned on both sides, about 5 minutes per side.

Add the chopped chipotle peppers, diced tomatoes (with their juices), dried oregano, ground cumin, smoked paprika, and chili powder to the skillet. Stir to combine.

Cover the skillet and simmer the chicken tinga over medium-low heat for 20-25 minutes, or until the chicken is cooked through and tender.

Remove the chicken from the skillet and shred it using two forks. Return the shredded chicken to the skillet and stir to coat it in the sauce.

Continue to simmer the chicken tinga uncovered for another 10-15 minutes, or until the sauce has thickened slightly.
Taste and adjust the seasoning with salt and pepper as needed.
Serve the Mexican Shredded Chicken Tinga with warm tortillas and your choice of toppings, such as chopped fresh cilantro, diced onion, crumbled queso fresco or shredded cheese, sliced avocado, and lime wedges.
Enjoy your delicious Mexican Shredded Chicken Tinga!

This Chicken Tinga recipe is perfect for a quick and flavorful meal that's sure to satisfy your Mexican food cravings. The tender shredded chicken in a smoky and spicy tomato sauce is versatile and can be used in a variety of dishes for a delicious and satisfying meal.

Main Courses - Seafood:

Fish Tacos in Lettuce Wraps with Cabbage Slaw

Ingredients:

For the Fish:

- 1 pound white fish fillets (such as tilapia, cod, or halibut)
- 1 tablespoon olive oil
- 1 teaspoon chili powder
- 1/2 teaspoon ground cumin
- 1/2 teaspoon smoked paprika
- Salt and pepper to taste
- Lettuce leaves (such as butter lettuce or romaine), for wrapping

For the Cabbage Slaw:

- 2 cups shredded cabbage (red or green, or a mix of both)
- 1/4 cup chopped fresh cilantro
- 1/4 cup chopped red onion
- 2 tablespoons mayonnaise
- 1 tablespoon lime juice
- 1 teaspoon honey or sugar
- Salt and pepper to taste

Optional Toppings:

- Sliced avocado
- Sliced jalapeños
- Salsa
- Sour cream or Greek yogurt
- Lime wedges

Instructions:

For the Fish:

> Preheat your oven to 375°F (190°C).
> Pat the fish fillets dry with paper towels and place them on a baking sheet lined with parchment paper or aluminum foil.

In a small bowl, mix together the olive oil, chili powder, ground cumin, smoked paprika, salt, and pepper. Brush the spice mixture over the fish fillets, coating them evenly.

Bake the fish in the preheated oven for 12-15 minutes, or until cooked through and easily flaked with a fork.

Once cooked, remove the fish from the oven and let it cool slightly before assembling the tacos.

For the Cabbage Slaw:

In a large bowl, combine the shredded cabbage, chopped cilantro, and chopped red onion.

In a small bowl, whisk together the mayonnaise, lime juice, honey or sugar, salt, and pepper to make the dressing.

Pour the dressing over the cabbage mixture and toss until evenly coated.

Assembling the Tacos:

Place a spoonful of the cabbage slaw onto each lettuce leaf.

Top the slaw with a piece of baked fish.

Add any optional toppings you like, such as sliced avocado, sliced jalapeños, salsa, sour cream or Greek yogurt, and a squeeze of lime juice.

Serve the fish tacos in lettuce wraps immediately, and enjoy!

These Fish Tacos in Lettuce Wraps with Cabbage Slaw are light, flavorful, and perfect for a healthy meal. They're also customizable, so feel free to add your favorite toppings or adjust the seasoning to suit your taste preferences.

Grilled Chipotle Lime Shrimp

Ingredients:

- 1 pound large shrimp, peeled and deveined
- 2 tablespoons olive oil
- Zest and juice of 1 lime
- 2 cloves garlic, minced
- 1 teaspoon chipotle chili powder
- 1/2 teaspoon smoked paprika
- 1/2 teaspoon ground cumin
- Salt and pepper to taste
- Chopped fresh cilantro for garnish
- Lime wedges for serving

Instructions:

In a bowl, combine the olive oil, lime zest, lime juice, minced garlic, chipotle chili powder, smoked paprika, ground cumin, salt, and pepper. Mix well to combine.
Add the peeled and deveined shrimp to the bowl with the marinade. Toss the shrimp until they are evenly coated with the marinade. Cover the bowl and let the shrimp marinate in the refrigerator for 15-30 minutes.
Preheat your grill to medium-high heat.
Thread the marinated shrimp onto skewers, leaving a little space between each shrimp.
Place the shrimp skewers on the preheated grill and cook for 2-3 minutes per side, or until the shrimp are pink and opaque.
Once cooked, remove the shrimp skewers from the grill and transfer them to a serving platter.
Garnish the grilled chipotle lime shrimp with chopped fresh cilantro and serve with lime wedges on the side.
Enjoy your delicious Grilled Chipotle Lime Shrimp as an appetizer or main course!

This dish is bursting with flavor from the chipotle chili powder, smoked paprika, and zesty lime juice. It's quick and easy to prepare, making it perfect for weeknight dinners or weekend cookouts. Serve the shrimp with rice, salad, or your favorite side dishes for a complete meal.

Baked Fish Veracruz Style

Ingredients:

- 4 fish fillets (such as red snapper, tilapia, or cod)
- Salt and pepper, to taste
- 2 tablespoons olive oil
- 1 onion, thinly sliced
- 2 cloves garlic, minced
- 1 bell pepper (any color), thinly sliced
- 1 can (14.5 ounces) diced tomatoes, drained
- 1/4 cup sliced green olives
- 2 tablespoons capers, drained
- 1 teaspoon dried oregano
- 1/2 teaspoon ground cumin
- 1/4 teaspoon red pepper flakes (optional, for heat)
- 1/4 cup chopped fresh cilantro
- Lime wedges, for serving

Instructions:

Preheat your oven to 375°F (190°C).
Season the fish fillets with salt and pepper on both sides. Place them in a baking dish lightly greased with olive oil.
In a skillet, heat the olive oil over medium heat. Add the sliced onion and cook until softened, about 5 minutes.
Add the minced garlic and sliced bell pepper to the skillet. Cook for another 2-3 minutes, until the vegetables are tender.
Stir in the drained diced tomatoes, sliced green olives, capers, dried oregano, ground cumin, and red pepper flakes (if using). Cook for 5 minutes, allowing the flavors to meld together.
Pour the tomato mixture over the fish fillets in the baking dish, covering them evenly.
Cover the baking dish with aluminum foil and bake in the preheated oven for 15-20 minutes, or until the fish is cooked through and flakes easily with a fork.
Once baked, remove the foil from the baking dish and sprinkle the chopped fresh cilantro over the fish.
Serve the Baked Fish Veracruz Style hot, garnished with lime wedges for squeezing over the fish.
Enjoy your flavorful and vibrant Baked Fish Veracruz Style!

This dish is perfect for a weeknight dinner or entertaining guests. The combination of tangy tomatoes, briny olives, and capers creates a delicious sauce that pairs beautifully with the tender and flaky fish. Serve it with rice, quinoa, or crusty bread to soak up the flavorful sauce.

Shrimp Enchiladas with Zucchini Tortillas

Ingredients:

For the Shrimp Filling:

- 1 pound shrimp, peeled and deveined
- 1 tablespoon olive oil
- 2 cloves garlic, minced
- 1 teaspoon ground cumin
- 1 teaspoon chili powder
- Salt and pepper to taste
- Juice of 1 lime
- 1/4 cup chopped fresh cilantro

For the Zucchini Tortillas:

- 3-4 large zucchini
- Olive oil for brushing
- Salt and pepper to taste

For the Enchilada Sauce:

- 1 tablespoon olive oil
- 1 onion, diced
- 2 cloves garlic, minced
- 1 can (14.5 ounces) diced tomatoes
- 1 can (4 ounces) diced green chilies
- 1 teaspoon ground cumin
- 1 teaspoon chili powder
- Salt and pepper to taste

For Assembly:

- 1 cup shredded cheese (such as Monterey Jack or cheddar)
- Chopped fresh cilantro for garnish
- Lime wedges for serving

Instructions:

For the Shrimp Filling:

Heat the olive oil in a skillet over medium heat. Add the minced garlic and cook for 1 minute until fragrant.

Add the shrimp to the skillet and season with ground cumin, chili powder, salt, and pepper. Cook for 2-3 minutes per side, or until the shrimp are pink and cooked through.

Remove the skillet from heat and squeeze lime juice over the cooked shrimp. Stir in chopped cilantro and set aside.

For the Zucchini Tortillas:

Preheat your oven to 375°F (190°C).

Slice the zucchini lengthwise into thin strips, about 1/8 inch thick, using a mandoline slicer or a sharp knife.

Place the zucchini strips on a baking sheet lined with parchment paper. Brush both sides of the zucchini slices with olive oil and season with salt and pepper.

Bake the zucchini slices in the preheated oven for 10-12 minutes, or until they are slightly softened. Remove from the oven and set aside.

For the Enchilada Sauce:

In a saucepan, heat olive oil over medium heat. Add diced onion and minced garlic and cook until softened, about 5 minutes.

Stir in diced tomatoes, diced green chilies, ground cumin, chili powder, salt, and pepper. Simmer for 10-15 minutes, stirring occasionally, until the sauce has thickened slightly. Remove the sauce from heat and set aside.

For Assembly:

Spread a thin layer of enchilada sauce on the bottom of a baking dish.

Place a spoonful of shrimp filling on each zucchini slice and roll up tightly.

Arrange the zucchini enchiladas in the baking dish, seam side down.

Pour the remaining enchilada sauce over the zucchini enchiladas, covering them evenly.

Sprinkle shredded cheese over the top of the enchiladas.

Bake in the preheated oven for 15-20 minutes, or until the cheese is melted and bubbly.

Garnish with chopped fresh cilantro and serve with lime wedges.

Enjoy your delicious Shrimp Enchiladas with Zucchini Tortillas!

These shrimp enchiladas with zucchini tortillas are flavorful, satisfying, and packed with nutritious ingredients. They're perfect for a lighter dinner option or for anyone looking to add more vegetables to their diet. Serve them with your favorite Mexican-inspired sides for a complete meal.

Mahi Mahi with Avocado Salsa

Ingredients:

For the Mahi Mahi:

- 4 mahi mahi fillets
- 2 tablespoons olive oil
- 1 teaspoon paprika
- 1 teaspoon ground cumin
- 1/2 teaspoon garlic powder
- Salt and pepper to taste
- Lime wedges for serving

For the Avocado Salsa:

- 2 ripe avocados, diced
- 1/2 cup cherry tomatoes, diced
- 1/4 cup red onion, finely chopped
- 1/4 cup fresh cilantro, chopped
- Juice of 1 lime
- Salt and pepper to taste

Instructions:

For the Mahi Mahi:

Preheat your grill to medium-high heat or preheat your oven to 375°F (190°C).

In a small bowl, mix together the olive oil, paprika, ground cumin, garlic powder, salt, and pepper to make a marinade.

Brush the mahi mahi fillets with the marinade on both sides.

If grilling: Place the mahi mahi fillets directly on the grill grates and cook for 4-5 minutes per side, or until the fish is cooked through and flakes easily with a fork.

If baking: Place the mahi mahi fillets on a baking sheet lined with parchment paper or aluminum foil. Bake in the preheated oven for 15-20 minutes, or until the fish is cooked through and flakes easily with a fork.

Once cooked, remove the mahi mahi fillets from the grill or oven and let them rest for a few minutes.

For the Avocado Salsa:

In a medium bowl, combine the diced avocado, cherry tomatoes, red onion, chopped cilantro, lime juice, salt, and pepper. Gently toss to combine.

Taste and adjust the seasoning with more salt, pepper, or lime juice if needed.

For Serving:

    Place the cooked mahi mahi fillets on serving plates.
    Spoon the avocado salsa generously over the top of each mahi mahi fillet.
    Garnish with additional chopped cilantro and serve with lime wedges on the side.
    Enjoy your delicious Mahi Mahi with Avocado Salsa!

This dish is perfect for a light and healthy dinner option that's full of flavor and nutrition. The tender and flaky mahi mahi pairs beautifully with the creamy and tangy avocado salsa, creating a delicious and satisfying meal. Serve it with your favorite sides, such as rice, quinoa, or a side salad, for a complete and balanced meal.

Main Courses - Vegetarian:

Portobello Mushroom Fajitas

Ingredients:

For the Portobello Mushrooms:

- 4 large portobello mushrooms, stems removed and sliced
- 2 tablespoons olive oil
- 2 cloves garlic, minced
- 1 teaspoon chili powder
- 1 teaspoon ground cumin
- 1/2 teaspoon smoked paprika
- Salt and pepper to taste

For the Fajita Vegetables:

- 1 onion, sliced
- 1 bell pepper (any color), sliced
- 1 tablespoon olive oil
- Salt and pepper to taste

For Serving:

- 8 small flour or corn tortillas
- Optional toppings: sliced avocado, shredded cheese, sour cream, salsa, chopped cilantro, lime wedges

Instructions:

For the Portobello Mushrooms:

In a large bowl, whisk together the olive oil, minced garlic, chili powder, ground cumin, smoked paprika, salt, and pepper.
Add the sliced portobello mushrooms to the bowl and toss until they are evenly coated with the marinade.
Let the mushrooms marinate for at least 15 minutes to allow the flavors to meld together.
Heat a large skillet or grill pan over medium-high heat. Add the marinated portobello mushrooms to the skillet in a single layer.

Cook the mushrooms for 3-4 minutes per side, or until they are tender and lightly browned. Remove them from the skillet and set aside.

For the Fajita Vegetables:

In the same skillet, heat another tablespoon of olive oil over medium-high heat.
Add the sliced onion and bell pepper to the skillet. Season with salt and pepper to taste.
Cook the vegetables, stirring occasionally, for 5-7 minutes, or until they are tender and slightly caramelized.
Once cooked, remove the skillet from the heat.

For Serving:

Warm the tortillas in a dry skillet or microwave according to package instructions.
Fill each tortilla with a portion of the cooked portobello mushrooms and fajita vegetables.
Add any optional toppings you like, such as sliced avocado, shredded cheese, sour cream, salsa, chopped cilantro, or a squeeze of lime juice.
Serve the Portobello Mushroom Fajitas immediately, and enjoy!

These fajitas are delicious, flavorful, and packed with nutritious ingredients. They're perfect for a quick and easy weeknight dinner or for entertaining guests. Customize them with your favorite toppings and enjoy a satisfying vegetarian meal!

Cauliflower Rice Stuffed Peppers

Ingredients:

For the Stuffed Peppers:

- 4 large bell peppers (any color), halved and seeds removed
- 1 tablespoon olive oil
- 1 small onion, diced
- 2 cloves garlic, minced
- 1 medium carrot, diced
- 1 stalk celery, diced
- 1 small zucchini, diced
- 2 cups cauliflower rice (store-bought or homemade)
- 1 can (14.5 ounces) diced tomatoes, drained
- 1 cup cooked black beans (or canned, drained and rinsed)
- 1 teaspoon ground cumin
- 1 teaspoon chili powder
- Salt and pepper to taste
- 1 cup shredded cheese (such as cheddar or Monterey Jack), divided
- Chopped fresh cilantro or parsley for garnish

Optional Toppings:

- Sliced avocado
- Sour cream or Greek yogurt
- Salsa

Instructions:

Preheat your oven to 375°F (190°C).

Heat the olive oil in a large skillet over medium heat. Add the diced onion and cook until softened, about 5 minutes.

Add the minced garlic, diced carrot, diced celery, and diced zucchini to the skillet. Cook, stirring occasionally, for another 5 minutes, or until the vegetables are tender.

Stir in the cauliflower rice, drained diced tomatoes, cooked black beans, ground cumin, chili powder, salt, and pepper. Cook for an additional 3-4 minutes, allowing the flavors to meld together.

Remove the skillet from the heat and stir in 1/2 cup of shredded cheese until melted and well combined.

Arrange the halved bell peppers in a baking dish, cut side up.

Spoon the cauliflower rice mixture evenly into each pepper half, pressing down gently to pack it in.

Cover the baking dish with aluminum foil and bake in the preheated oven for 25-30 minutes, or until the peppers are tender.

Remove the foil from the baking dish and sprinkle the remaining 1/2 cup of shredded cheese over the top of the stuffed peppers.

Return the baking dish to the oven and bake for an additional 5-10 minutes, or until the cheese is melted and bubbly.

Once cooked, remove the stuffed peppers from the oven and let them cool slightly.

Garnish the stuffed peppers with chopped fresh cilantro or parsley.

Serve the Cauliflower Rice Stuffed Peppers hot, with optional toppings such as sliced avocado, sour cream or Greek yogurt, and salsa on the side.

Enjoy your delicious and nutritious Cauliflower Rice Stuffed Peppers!

These stuffed peppers are packed with flavor and nutrients, making them a perfect option for a wholesome weeknight dinner. They're also great for meal prep and can be easily customized with your favorite vegetables and toppings.

Vegetarian Enchiladas with Black Beans and Cheese

Ingredients:

For the Enchilada Filling:

- 1 can (15 ounces) black beans, drained and rinsed
- 1 cup corn kernels (fresh, frozen, or canned)
- 1 bell pepper, diced
- 1 small onion, diced
- 2 cloves garlic, minced
- 1 teaspoon ground cumin
- 1 teaspoon chili powder
- Salt and pepper to taste
- 2 cups shredded cheese (such as cheddar or Monterey Jack), divided
- 1/4 cup chopped fresh cilantro
- 8 large flour or corn tortillas

For the Enchilada Sauce:

- 2 tablespoons olive oil
- 2 tablespoons all-purpose flour (or cornstarch for gluten-free)
- 2 tablespoons chili powder
- 1 teaspoon ground cumin
- 1/2 teaspoon garlic powder
- 1/4 teaspoon dried oregano
- 1/4 teaspoon salt
- 1 can (14.5 ounces) diced tomatoes
- 1 1/2 cups vegetable broth

Optional Toppings:

- Sliced avocado
- Chopped fresh cilantro
- Sour cream or Greek yogurt
- Sliced jalapeños
- Lime wedges

Instructions:

For the Enchilada Filling:

Preheat your oven to 375°F (190°C). Grease a 9x13-inch baking dish with cooking spray and set aside.

In a large skillet, heat a tablespoon of olive oil over medium heat. Add the diced onion and bell pepper, and cook until softened, about 5 minutes.

Add the minced garlic, ground cumin, chili powder, salt, and pepper to the skillet. Cook for an additional minute until fragrant.

Stir in the drained black beans and corn kernels, and cook for another 2-3 minutes until heated through. Remove the skillet from heat and let the mixture cool slightly.

Once cooled, stir in 1 cup of shredded cheese and chopped cilantro into the black bean and corn mixture.

For the Enchilada Sauce:

In a saucepan, heat 2 tablespoons of olive oil over medium heat. Stir in the flour (or cornstarch) and cook for 1-2 minutes to make a roux.

Add the chili powder, ground cumin, garlic powder, dried oregano, and salt to the roux. Cook for another minute, stirring constantly.

Slowly pour in the diced tomatoes and vegetable broth, whisking continuously to prevent lumps from forming.

Bring the sauce to a simmer and cook for 5-7 minutes, stirring occasionally, until the sauce has thickened slightly. Remove from heat and set aside.

Assembling the Enchiladas:

Spread a small amount of enchilada sauce on the bottom of the greased baking dish.

Place a tortilla on a flat surface, and spoon some of the black bean and corn filling down the center of the tortilla. Roll it up tightly and place it seam-side down in the baking dish.

Repeat with the remaining tortillas and filling, arranging them snugly in the baking dish.

Pour the remaining enchilada sauce evenly over the top of the assembled enchiladas.

Sprinkle the remaining shredded cheese on top of the enchiladas.

Cover the baking dish with aluminum foil and bake in the preheated oven for 20-25 minutes, or until the enchiladas are heated through and the cheese is melted and bubbly.

Once cooked, remove the foil from the baking dish and let the enchiladas cool slightly before serving.

Serving:

> Serve the Vegetarian Enchiladas with Black Beans and Cheese hot, garnished with optional toppings such as sliced avocado, chopped fresh cilantro, sour cream or Greek yogurt, sliced jalapeños, and lime wedges.
> Enjoy your delicious and flavorful vegetarian enchiladas!

These enchiladas are a fantastic option for a meatless dinner that's packed with protein and flavor. They're sure to be a hit with vegetarians and meat-eaters alike!

Mexican Zucchini Boats with Ground Tofu

Ingredients:

For the Zucchini Boats:

- 4 large zucchini
- 1 tablespoon olive oil
- 1 onion, diced
- 2 cloves garlic, minced
- 1 bell pepper (any color), diced
- 1 jalapeño pepper, seeded and diced (optional, for heat)
- 1 package (14 ounces) extra-firm tofu, crumbled
- 1 can (14.5 ounces) diced tomatoes, drained
- 1 cup cooked black beans (or canned, drained and rinsed)
- 1 teaspoon ground cumin
- 1 teaspoon chili powder
- Salt and pepper to taste
- 1/2 cup shredded cheese (such as cheddar or Monterey Jack)
- Chopped fresh cilantro for garnish

Optional Toppings:

- Sliced avocado
- Sour cream or Greek yogurt
- Salsa
- Lime wedges

Instructions:

Preheat your oven to 375°F (190°C). Lightly grease a baking dish with olive oil or non-stick cooking spray.

Cut each zucchini in half lengthwise, then use a spoon to scoop out the seeds and create a hollow "boat." Place the hollowed-out zucchini halves in the prepared baking dish.

In a large skillet, heat the olive oil over medium heat. Add the diced onion and cook until softened, about 5 minutes.

Add the minced garlic, diced bell pepper, and diced jalapeño pepper (if using) to the skillet. Cook for another 2-3 minutes, until the vegetables are tender.

Add the crumbled tofu to the skillet and cook for 5-7 minutes, stirring occasionally, until the tofu is lightly browned.

Stir in the drained diced tomatoes, cooked black beans, ground cumin, chili powder, salt, and pepper. Cook for another 3-4 minutes, allowing the flavors to meld together.

Spoon the tofu and vegetable mixture evenly into the hollowed-out zucchini halves, filling them to the top.

Sprinkle shredded cheese over the top of each zucchini boat.

Cover the baking dish with aluminum foil and bake in the preheated oven for 20-25 minutes, or until the zucchini is tender.

Once cooked, remove the foil from the baking dish and broil the zucchini boats for an additional 2-3 minutes, or until the cheese is melted and bubbly.

Remove the zucchini boats from the oven and let them cool slightly.

Garnish the Mexican Zucchini Boats with chopped fresh cilantro and serve with optional toppings such as sliced avocado, sour cream or Greek yogurt, salsa, and lime wedges on the side.

Enjoy your flavorful and nutritious Mexican Zucchini Boats with Ground Tofu!

These zucchini boats are packed with protein, fiber, and flavor, making them a satisfying vegetarian meal option. They're perfect for a quick and easy weeknight dinner or for entertaining guests. Customize them with your favorite toppings and enjoy a delicious and wholesome meal!

Veggie Fajita Bowls with Guacamole and Sour Cream

Ingredients:

For the Veggie Fajitas:

- 2 bell peppers (any color), sliced
- 1 large onion, sliced
- 2 tablespoons olive oil
- 1 teaspoon ground cumin
- 1 teaspoon chili powder
- 1/2 teaspoon smoked paprika
- Salt and pepper to taste

For the Guacamole:

- 2 ripe avocados
- 1/4 cup diced red onion
- 1/4 cup chopped fresh cilantro
- 1 small jalapeño pepper, seeded and minced (optional, for heat)
- Juice of 1 lime
- Salt and pepper to taste

For Serving:

- Cooked rice or quinoa
- Black beans, drained and rinsed
- Sour cream or Greek yogurt
- Lime wedges
- Chopped fresh cilantro for garnish

Instructions:

For the Veggie Fajitas:

> Heat 1 tablespoon of olive oil in a large skillet over medium-high heat.
> Add the sliced bell peppers and onion to the skillet. Season with ground cumin, chili powder, smoked paprika, salt, and pepper.
> Cook the vegetables, stirring occasionally, for 8-10 minutes, or until they are tender and slightly caramelized.
> Once cooked, remove the skillet from the heat and set aside.

For the Guacamole:

    Cut the avocados in half and remove the pits. Scoop the avocado flesh into a bowl.
    Add the diced red onion, chopped fresh cilantro, minced jalapeño pepper (if using), and lime juice to the bowl with the avocado.
    Mash everything together with a fork until the guacamole reaches your desired consistency. Season with salt and pepper to taste.
    Once prepared, set the guacamole aside.

For Serving:

    Divide the cooked rice or quinoa among serving bowls.
    Top the rice or quinoa with a portion of the cooked veggie fajitas and black beans.
    Add a dollop of guacamole and sour cream or Greek yogurt to each bowl.
    Garnish with chopped fresh cilantro and serve with lime wedges on the side.
    Enjoy your delicious Veggie Fajita Bowls with Guacamole and Sour Cream!

These fajita bowls are customizable and perfect for a quick and healthy weeknight dinner. They're also great for meal prep and can be easily customized with your favorite toppings and additions. Enjoy the flavorful combination of tender veggies, creamy guacamole, and tangy sour cream in every bite!

Side Dishes:

Mexican Cauliflower Rice

Ingredients:

- 1 large head of cauliflower, riced (about 4-5 cups)
- 2 tablespoons olive oil
- 1 onion, finely diced
- 2 cloves garlic, minced
- 1 bell pepper, finely diced
- 1 jalapeño pepper, seeded and finely diced (optional, for heat)
- 1 teaspoon ground cumin
- 1 teaspoon chili powder
- 1/2 teaspoon smoked paprika
- 1/4 teaspoon cayenne pepper (optional, for extra heat)
- Salt and pepper to taste
- 1/4 cup chopped fresh cilantro
- Juice of 1 lime

Instructions:

Start by preparing the cauliflower rice. Cut the cauliflower into florets and place them in a food processor. Pulse until the cauliflower resembles rice-like grains. You may need to work in batches depending on the size of your food processor. Alternatively, you can grate the cauliflower using a box grater.

Heat the olive oil in a large skillet over medium heat. Add the diced onion and cook until softened, about 5 minutes.

Add the minced garlic, diced bell pepper, and diced jalapeño pepper (if using) to the skillet. Cook for another 2-3 minutes, until the vegetables are tender.

Stir in the riced cauliflower, ground cumin, chili powder, smoked paprika, and cayenne pepper (if using). Season with salt and pepper to taste.

Cook the cauliflower rice mixture, stirring occasionally, for 5-7 minutes, or until the cauliflower is tender but still slightly crisp.

Once cooked, remove the skillet from the heat and stir in the chopped fresh cilantro and lime juice. Taste and adjust the seasoning if needed.

Serve the Mexican Cauliflower Rice hot as a side dish or as a base for your favorite Mexican-inspired recipes.

Enjoy your flavorful and nutritious Mexican Cauliflower Rice!

This Mexican Cauliflower Rice is versatile and can be used in various dishes such as burrito bowls, tacos, enchiladas, or served alongside grilled meats or seafood. It's a delicious way to incorporate more vegetables into your diet while still enjoying the flavors of Mexican cuisine.

Charred Mexican Street Corn (Elote) with Lime Crema

Ingredients:

For the Charred Mexican Street Corn (Elote):

- 4 ears of corn, husked
- 2 tablespoons mayonnaise
- 2 tablespoons sour cream or Greek yogurt
- 1/4 cup crumbled cotija cheese (or feta cheese)
- 1 teaspoon chili powder
- 1/2 teaspoon smoked paprika
- 1/4 teaspoon cayenne pepper (optional, for extra heat)
- Salt and pepper to taste
- Chopped fresh cilantro for garnish
- Lime wedges for serving

For the Lime Crema:

- 1/4 cup sour cream or Greek yogurt
- Juice of 1 lime
- 1 teaspoon lime zest
- Salt to taste

Instructions:

For the Charred Mexican Street Corn (Elote):

Preheat your grill to medium-high heat.
Place the husked ears of corn directly on the grill grates. Cook the corn, turning occasionally, until it is charred and slightly tender, about 10-12 minutes.
In a small bowl, mix together the mayonnaise, sour cream or Greek yogurt, crumbled cotija cheese, chili powder, smoked paprika, cayenne pepper (if using), salt, and pepper.
Once the corn is cooked, remove it from the grill and let it cool slightly.
Spread the mayonnaise mixture evenly over each ear of corn, coating it generously.
Garnish the charred Mexican street corn with chopped fresh cilantro and serve with lime wedges on the side.

For the Lime Crema:

In a small bowl, whisk together the sour cream or Greek yogurt, lime juice, lime zest, and salt until smooth and creamy.

Taste and adjust the seasoning with more salt or lime juice if needed.

For Serving:

Drizzle the Lime Crema over the charred Mexican street corn just before serving, or serve it on the side for dipping.
Enjoy your delicious Charred Mexican Street Corn (Elote) with Lime Crema as a flavorful and zesty side dish or appetizer!

This dish is bursting with flavor from the charred corn, creamy mayonnaise mixture, and zesty lime crema. It's a popular street food in Mexico and is sure to be a hit at your next barbecue or gathering. Serve it alongside grilled meats, tacos, or as part of a Mexican-themed meal for a delicious and memorable dish.

Avocado and Tomato Salad with Cilantro Lime Vinaigrette

Ingredients:

For the Salad:

- 2 ripe avocados, diced
- 2 large tomatoes, diced
- 1/4 cup red onion, finely chopped
- 1/4 cup chopped fresh cilantro
- Salt and pepper to taste
- Optional: crumbled feta cheese or queso fresco for garnish

For the Cilantro Lime Vinaigrette:

- 1/4 cup fresh lime juice (about 2-3 limes)
- 1/4 cup extra virgin olive oil
- 2 tablespoons chopped fresh cilantro
- 1 teaspoon honey or sugar (optional, to balance acidity)
- 1 clove garlic, minced
- Salt and pepper to taste

Instructions:

For the Cilantro Lime Vinaigrette:

In a small bowl, whisk together the fresh lime juice, extra virgin olive oil, chopped cilantro, minced garlic, honey or sugar (if using), salt, and pepper until well combined.
Taste the vinaigrette and adjust the seasoning or sweetness to your liking. Set aside.

For the Salad:

In a large mixing bowl, combine the diced avocado, diced tomatoes, finely chopped red onion, and chopped fresh cilantro.
Season the salad with salt and pepper to taste.
Drizzle the cilantro lime vinaigrette over the salad ingredients, starting with about half of the dressing, and toss gently to coat.
Taste the salad and add more dressing as needed, depending on your preference.
Optional: Garnish the salad with crumbled feta cheese or queso fresco for added flavor and texture.
Serve the Avocado and Tomato Salad with Cilantro Lime Vinaigrette immediately as a side dish or light lunch.

Enjoy the fresh and vibrant flavors of this delicious salad!

This Avocado and Tomato Salad with Cilantro Lime Vinaigrette is perfect for summer gatherings, picnics, or as a light and healthy meal any time of the year. The creamy avocado, juicy tomatoes, and tangy vinaigrette create a delicious flavor combination that's sure to impress.

Sautéed Garlic Spinach with Cotija Cheese

Ingredients:

- 1 tablespoon olive oil
- 2 cloves garlic, minced
- 8 cups fresh spinach leaves, washed and dried
- Salt and pepper to taste
- 1/4 cup crumbled cotija cheese
- Lime wedges for serving (optional)

Instructions:

> Heat the olive oil in a large skillet over medium heat.
> Add the minced garlic to the skillet and sauté for 1-2 minutes, or until fragrant.
> Add the fresh spinach leaves to the skillet in batches, stirring frequently, until all the spinach is wilted. This should take about 3-4 minutes.
> Season the sautéed spinach with salt and pepper to taste, and continue cooking for another 1-2 minutes, stirring occasionally.
> Once the spinach is cooked and seasoned to your liking, remove the skillet from the heat.
> Transfer the sautéed garlic spinach to a serving dish.
> Sprinkle the crumbled cotija cheese evenly over the top of the spinach.
> Serve the sautéed garlic spinach with cotija cheese immediately, with lime wedges on the side for squeezing over the top if desired.
> Enjoy your delicious and nutritious side dish!

This Sautéed Garlic Spinach with Cotija Cheese is quick and easy to prepare, making it perfect for busy weeknights or whenever you need a simple yet flavorful side dish. The combination of garlic, spinach, and tangy cotija cheese creates a delicious flavor profile that's sure to please.

Grilled Mexican Squash with Chili and Lime

Ingredients:

- 4 medium Mexican squash (also known as calabacitas or zucchini), sliced lengthwise into halves
- 2 tablespoons olive oil
- 2 cloves garlic, minced
- 1 teaspoon chili powder
- 1/2 teaspoon ground cumin
- 1/4 teaspoon smoked paprika
- Salt and pepper to taste
- Juice of 1 lime
- Chopped fresh cilantro for garnish
- Lime wedges for serving

Instructions:

Preheat your grill to medium-high heat.
In a small bowl, whisk together the olive oil, minced garlic, chili powder, ground cumin, smoked paprika, salt, and pepper.
Brush both sides of the sliced Mexican squash with the prepared olive oil mixture.
Place the squash slices on the preheated grill and cook for 3-4 minutes per side, or until they are tender and grill marks appear.
Once the squash is cooked, remove it from the grill and transfer it to a serving platter.
Drizzle the grilled Mexican squash with fresh lime juice.
Garnish with chopped fresh cilantro.
Serve the grilled Mexican squash with chili and lime immediately, with lime wedges on the side for squeezing over the top if desired.
Enjoy your delicious and flavorful side dish!

This Grilled Mexican Squash with Chili and Lime is perfect for summer barbecues, picnics, or any time you want to add a burst of flavor to your meal. The combination of chili, lime, and grilled squash creates a delicious and satisfying dish that's sure to impress.

Main Courses - Vegetarian:

Mexican Cauliflower Rice

Ingredients:

- 1 large head of cauliflower, riced (about 4-5 cups)
- 2 tablespoons olive oil
- 1 small onion, finely chopped
- 2 cloves garlic, minced
- 1 bell pepper (any color), diced
- 1 jalapeño pepper, seeded and minced (optional, for heat)
- 1 teaspoon ground cumin
- 1 teaspoon chili powder
- 1/2 teaspoon smoked paprika
- Salt and pepper to taste
- 1/4 cup chopped fresh cilantro
- Juice of 1 lime

Instructions:

Start by preparing the cauliflower rice. Cut the cauliflower into florets and place them in a food processor. Pulse until the cauliflower resembles rice-like grains. You may need to work in batches depending on the size of your food processor. Alternatively, you can grate the cauliflower using a box grater.
Heat the olive oil in a large skillet over medium heat.
Add the chopped onion to the skillet and cook until it becomes translucent, about 3-4 minutes.
Add the minced garlic, diced bell pepper, and minced jalapeño pepper (if using) to the skillet. Cook for another 2-3 minutes until the vegetables are tender.
Stir in the cauliflower rice, ground cumin, chili powder, smoked paprika, salt, and pepper. Cook for about 5-7 minutes, stirring occasionally, until the cauliflower is tender but still slightly crisp.
Once cooked, remove the skillet from the heat and stir in the chopped fresh cilantro and lime juice.
Taste and adjust the seasoning if needed.
Serve the Mexican Cauliflower Rice as a side dish alongside your favorite Mexican-inspired main courses.
Enjoy your flavorful and nutritious Mexican Cauliflower Rice!

This dish is packed with flavor from the spices and fresh herbs, making it a perfect accompaniment to tacos, fajitas, burrito bowls, or as a filling for stuffed peppers. It's a great way to enjoy the flavors of Mexican cuisine while keeping your meal low-carb and healthy.

Charred Mexican Street Corn (Elote) with Lime Crema

Ingredients:

For the Charred Mexican Street Corn (Elote):

- 4 ears of corn, husked
- 2 tablespoons mayonnaise
- 2 tablespoons sour cream or Mexican crema
- 1/4 cup crumbled cotija cheese
- 1 teaspoon chili powder
- 1/4 teaspoon smoked paprika
- 1 clove garlic, minced
- Salt and pepper to taste
- Lime wedges, for serving
- Chopped fresh cilantro, for garnish

For the Lime Crema:

- 1/4 cup sour cream or Greek yogurt
- Juice of 1 lime
- 1 teaspoon lime zest
- Salt to taste

Instructions:

For the Lime Crema:

In a small bowl, whisk together the sour cream or Greek yogurt, lime juice, lime zest, and a pinch of salt until smooth and creamy. Set aside.

For the Charred Mexican Street Corn:

Preheat your grill to medium-high heat.
In a small bowl, combine the mayonnaise, sour cream or Mexican crema, crumbled cotija cheese, chili powder, smoked paprika, minced garlic, salt, and pepper. Mix until well combined to make the elote topping.
Place the husked ears of corn directly onto the grill grates. Grill the corn, turning occasionally, until it is charred and cooked through, about 10-12 minutes.
Once the corn is cooked, remove it from the grill and place it on a serving platter.
Use a brush or spoon to generously slather each ear of corn with the elote topping, coating it evenly on all sides.

Garnish the charred Mexican street corn with chopped fresh cilantro.
Serve the corn immediately with lime wedges on the side and the prepared lime crema for drizzling over the top.
Enjoy your delicious Charred Mexican Street Corn (Elote) with Lime Crema!

This dish is bursting with flavor from the creamy elote topping, zesty lime crema, and charred corn. It's a popular street food in Mexico and is sure to be a hit at your next barbecue or gathering. Serve it as a side dish or appetizer alongside your favorite Mexican-inspired dishes for a memorable and delicious meal.

Avocado and Tomato Salad with Cilantro Lime Vinaigrette

Ingredients:

For the Salad:

- 2 large ripe avocados, diced
- 2 large ripe tomatoes, diced
- 1/4 cup red onion, finely diced
- 1/4 cup fresh cilantro, chopped
- Salt and pepper to taste

For the Cilantro Lime Vinaigrette:

- 1/4 cup fresh lime juice (about 2-3 limes)
- 1/4 cup extra virgin olive oil
- 2 tablespoons fresh cilantro, chopped
- 1 clove garlic, minced
- 1 teaspoon honey or maple syrup (optional)
- Salt and pepper to taste

Instructions:

For the Cilantro Lime Vinaigrette:

In a small bowl, whisk together the lime juice, olive oil, chopped cilantro, minced garlic, honey or maple syrup (if using), salt, and pepper until well combined. Set aside.

For the Avocado and Tomato Salad:

In a large mixing bowl, combine the diced avocados, diced tomatoes, finely diced red onion, and chopped cilantro.
Season the salad with salt and pepper to taste.
Drizzle the cilantro lime vinaigrette over the salad ingredients, starting with about half of the dressing, and toss gently to coat.
Taste the salad and add more dressing if desired.
Serve the avocado and tomato salad immediately as a side dish or light lunch.
Enjoy your delicious and refreshing Avocado and Tomato Salad with Cilantro Lime Vinaigrette!

This salad is perfect for picnics, barbecues, or as a fresh and healthy side dish for any meal. The combination of creamy avocado, juicy tomatoes, tangy red onion, and zesty cilantro lime vinaigrette creates a burst of flavor in every bite.

Sautéed Garlic Spinach with Cotija Cheese

Ingredients:

- 1 tablespoon olive oil
- 2 cloves garlic, minced
- 8 cups fresh spinach leaves, washed and dried
- Salt and pepper to taste
- 1/4 cup crumbled cotija cheese (or feta cheese)
- Optional: Lime wedges for serving

Instructions:

Heat the olive oil in a large skillet over medium heat.
Add the minced garlic to the skillet and sauté for 1-2 minutes, or until fragrant.
Add the fresh spinach leaves to the skillet in batches, stirring frequently, until all the spinach is wilted. This should take about 3-4 minutes.
Season the sautéed spinach with salt and pepper to taste, and continue cooking for another 1-2 minutes, stirring occasionally.
Once the spinach is cooked, transfer it to a serving dish.
Sprinkle the crumbled cotija cheese evenly over the top of the spinach.
Serve the sautéed garlic spinach with cotija cheese immediately, with lime wedges on the side for squeezing over the top if desired.
Enjoy your delicious and nutritious side dish!

This Sautéed Garlic Spinach with Cotija Cheese is a versatile dish that pairs well with a variety of main courses. It's perfect for adding a pop of flavor and color to your meal, and it's sure to become a favorite in your recipe rotation.

Grilled Mexican Squash with Chili and Lime

Ingredients:

- 4 medium Mexican squash (also known as calabacitas or zucchini), sliced lengthwise into halves
- 2 tablespoons olive oil
- 1 teaspoon chili powder
- 1/2 teaspoon ground cumin
- 1/4 teaspoon smoked paprika
- Salt and pepper to taste
- Juice of 1 lime
- Optional: Chopped fresh cilantro for garnish

Instructions:

Preheat your grill to medium-high heat.
In a small bowl, whisk together the olive oil, chili powder, ground cumin, smoked paprika, salt, and pepper.
Brush both sides of the sliced Mexican squash with the prepared olive oil mixture.
Place the squash slices on the preheated grill and cook for 3-4 minutes per side, or until they are tender and grill marks appear.
Once the squash is cooked, remove it from the grill and transfer it to a serving platter.
Drizzle the grilled Mexican squash with fresh lime juice.
Optional: Garnish with chopped fresh cilantro for added flavor and freshness.
Serve the grilled Mexican squash with chili and lime immediately as a side dish or appetizer.
Enjoy your delicious and flavorful Grilled Mexican Squash with Chili and Lime!

This dish is perfect for summer gatherings or weeknight dinners. The combination of smoky grilled squash with zesty lime and warm spices creates a delicious flavor profile that pairs well with a variety of main courses. It's sure to be a hit with family and friends!

Salsas and Sauces:

Pico de Gallo

Ingredients:

- 4 ripe tomatoes, diced
- 1/2 onion, finely chopped
- 1 jalapeño pepper, seeded and finely chopped
- 1/4 cup fresh cilantro, chopped
- Juice of 1 lime
- Salt to taste

Instructions:

In a mixing bowl, combine the diced tomatoes, finely chopped onion, chopped jalapeño pepper, and chopped cilantro.
Squeeze the juice of one lime over the mixture.
Season with salt to taste.
Gently toss all the ingredients together until well combined.
Taste and adjust the seasoning, adding more lime juice or salt if needed.
Let the Pico de Gallo sit at room temperature for about 15-30 minutes to allow the flavors to meld together.
Serve the Pico de Gallo as a topping for tacos, nachos, quesadillas, grilled meats, or enjoy it with tortilla chips as a refreshing appetizer.
Store any leftovers in an airtight container in the refrigerator for up to 2-3 days.

Enjoy the fresh and zesty flavors of homemade Pico de Gallo! Adjust the ingredients according to your preference for spiciness and acidity, and feel free to customize it by adding diced avocado or mango for a unique twist.

Tomatillo Salsa Verde

Ingredients:

- 1 pound tomatillos, husks removed and rinsed
- 1 onion, quartered
- 2 cloves garlic
- 1 jalapeño pepper, stemmed and seeded (adjust to taste for desired spiciness)
- 1/4 cup fresh cilantro leaves
- Juice of 1 lime
- Salt to taste

Instructions:

Preheat the broiler in your oven.
Place the tomatillos, quartered onion, garlic cloves, and jalapeño pepper on a baking sheet lined with parchment paper.
Broil the vegetables for 5-7 minutes, or until they are charred and softened, turning them halfway through the cooking time.
Remove the baking sheet from the oven and let the vegetables cool slightly.
Transfer the roasted vegetables to a blender or food processor.
Add the fresh cilantro leaves and lime juice to the blender.
Blend the mixture until smooth, adding a little water if needed to reach your desired consistency.
Season the salsa verde with salt to taste, and blend again to combine.
Taste the salsa and adjust the seasoning or add more lime juice if desired.
Transfer the salsa verde to a serving bowl.
Serve the tomatillo salsa verde as a dip with tortilla chips, or use it as a sauce for tacos, enchiladas, grilled meats, or other Mexican dishes.
Store any leftovers in an airtight container in the refrigerator for up to 5 days.

Enjoy the bright and tangy flavors of homemade Tomatillo Salsa Verde! Adjust the amount of jalapeño pepper according to your desired level of spiciness, and feel free to customize the salsa with additional ingredients such as roasted poblano peppers or avocado for extra creaminess.

Roasted Red Pepper Salsa

Ingredients:

- 2 large red bell peppers
- 2 tomatoes
- 1/2 onion, roughly chopped
- 2 cloves garlic, peeled
- 1 jalapeño pepper, seeded and chopped (adjust to taste for desired spiciness)
- Juice of 1 lime
- 1/4 cup fresh cilantro leaves
- Salt and pepper to taste

Instructions:

Preheat the broiler in your oven.
Place the red bell peppers and tomatoes on a baking sheet lined with parchment paper.
Broil the vegetables for 8-10 minutes, or until the skins are charred and blistered, turning them occasionally to ensure even cooking.
Remove the baking sheet from the oven and let the vegetables cool slightly.
Once the vegetables are cool enough to handle, peel off the charred skins from the red bell peppers and tomatoes.
Remove the seeds and membranes from the red bell peppers and roughly chop them.
Transfer the roasted red bell peppers and peeled tomatoes to a blender or food processor.
Add the roughly chopped onion, garlic cloves, chopped jalapeño pepper, lime juice, and fresh cilantro leaves to the blender.
Blend the mixture until smooth, adding a little water if needed to reach your desired consistency.
Season the salsa with salt and pepper to taste, and blend again to combine.
Taste the salsa and adjust the seasoning or add more lime juice if desired.
Transfer the roasted red pepper salsa to a serving bowl.
Serve the salsa as a dip with tortilla chips, or use it as a sauce for tacos, quesadillas, grilled meats, or other dishes.
Store any leftovers in an airtight container in the refrigerator for up to 5 days.

Enjoy the smoky sweetness of homemade Roasted Red Pepper Salsa! You can adjust the level of spiciness by adding more or less jalapeño pepper, and feel free to customize the salsa with additional ingredients such as roasted garlic or chipotle peppers for extra flavor.

Chipotle Lime Crema

Ingredients:

- 1/2 cup sour cream
- 2 tablespoons mayonnaise
- 1 chipotle pepper in adobo sauce, minced
- 1 tablespoon adobo sauce (from the can of chipotle peppers)
- Juice of 1 lime
- 1 teaspoon lime zest
- 1 clove garlic, minced
- Salt to taste

Instructions:

In a small bowl, combine the sour cream, mayonnaise, minced chipotle pepper, adobo sauce, lime juice, lime zest, and minced garlic.
Stir the ingredients together until well combined.
Taste the chipotle lime crema and add salt as needed to suit your taste preferences.
Cover the bowl with plastic wrap or transfer the chipotle lime crema to an airtight container.
Refrigerate the crema for at least 30 minutes to allow the flavors to meld together.
Serve the chipotle lime crema as a dipping sauce for tacos, quesadillas, nachos, or as a topping for grilled meats, seafood, or vegetables.
Store any leftover chipotle lime crema in an airtight container in the refrigerator for up to 5 days.

Enjoy the creamy, tangy, and smoky flavors of homemade Chipotle Lime Crema! Adjust the amount of chipotle pepper and adobo sauce according to your desired level of spiciness, and feel free to customize the crema with additional ingredients such as cilantro or cumin for extra flavor.

Avocado Crema

Ingredients:

- 2 ripe avocados, peeled and pitted
- 1/2 cup sour cream or Greek yogurt
- Juice of 1 lime
- 1 clove garlic, minced
- Salt and pepper to taste
- Optional: chopped fresh cilantro, chopped jalapeño, or hot sauce for added flavor

Instructions:

In a blender or food processor, combine the peeled and pitted avocados, sour cream or Greek yogurt, lime juice, minced garlic, salt, and pepper.

Blend the ingredients until smooth and creamy. If the mixture is too thick, you can add a little water or additional lime juice to reach your desired consistency.

Taste the avocado crema and adjust the seasoning as needed, adding more salt, pepper, or lime juice to suit your taste preferences.

Optional: Stir in chopped fresh cilantro, chopped jalapeño, or a few dashes of hot sauce for added flavor and heat.

Transfer the avocado crema to a serving bowl.

Serve the avocado crema as a dipping sauce for tacos, quesadillas, nachos, or as a topping for grilled meats, seafood, or vegetables.

Store any leftover avocado crema in an airtight container in the refrigerator for up to 2 days. To prevent browning, press plastic wrap directly onto the surface of the crema before sealing the container.

Enjoy the creamy and delicious flavors of homemade Avocado Crema! It adds a delightful richness and tanginess to a variety of dishes, making it a versatile and tasty condiment for any occasion.

Snacks:

Spicy Mexican Roasted Nuts

Ingredients:

- 2 cups mixed nuts (such as almonds, cashews, peanuts, and pecans)
- 1 tablespoon olive oil or melted butter
- 1 tablespoon chili powder
- 1 teaspoon smoked paprika
- 1/2 teaspoon ground cumin
- 1/4 teaspoon cayenne pepper (adjust to taste for desired level of spiciness)
- 1/2 teaspoon garlic powder
- 1/2 teaspoon onion powder
- 1/2 teaspoon salt (adjust to taste)
- 1 tablespoon honey or maple syrup (optional, for sweetness)
- Fresh cilantro, chopped (for garnish, optional)

Instructions:

Preheat your oven to 325°F (160°C) and line a baking sheet with parchment paper or aluminum foil.

In a large mixing bowl, combine the mixed nuts, olive oil or melted butter, chili powder, smoked paprika, ground cumin, cayenne pepper, garlic powder, onion powder, salt, and honey or maple syrup (if using). Toss until the nuts are evenly coated with the spice mixture.

Spread the seasoned nuts in a single layer on the prepared baking sheet.

Roast the nuts in the preheated oven for 15-20 minutes, stirring halfway through, until they are toasted and fragrant. Keep an eye on them to prevent burning.

Remove the baking sheet from the oven and let the nuts cool completely on the pan.

Once cooled, transfer the spicy Mexican roasted nuts to a serving bowl.

Garnish with fresh chopped cilantro if desired.

Serve the spicy Mexican roasted nuts as a snack or appetizer for parties, game nights, or gatherings.

Store any leftover nuts in an airtight container at room temperature for up to one week.

Enjoy the crunchy, spicy, and flavorful goodness of homemade Spicy Mexican Roasted Nuts! Adjust the amount of cayenne pepper according to your preferred level of heat, and feel free to customize the spice blend with your favorite Mexican-inspired seasonings.

Queso Fundido with Chorizo and Bell Peppers (sans tortillas)

Ingredients:

- 8 oz (225g) Mexican chorizo, casing removed
- 1 tablespoon olive oil
- 1 small onion, diced
- 1 bell pepper (any color), diced
- 2 cloves garlic, minced
- 8 oz (225g) Monterey Jack cheese, shredded
- 4 oz (115g) sharp cheddar cheese, shredded
- 1 jalapeño pepper, thinly sliced (optional, for extra heat)
- Chopped fresh cilantro, for garnish (optional)
- Sliced avocado, for serving (optional)

Instructions:

Preheat your oven to 375°F (190°C).

In a large skillet, cook the Mexican chorizo over medium heat, breaking it apart with a spoon, until it is browned and cooked through, about 5-7 minutes. Remove the cooked chorizo from the skillet and set it aside.

In the same skillet, heat the olive oil over medium heat. Add the diced onion and bell pepper, and cook until they are softened, about 5 minutes.

Add the minced garlic to the skillet and cook for an additional 1-2 minutes, until fragrant.

Return the cooked chorizo to the skillet and stir to combine with the vegetables.

Sprinkle the shredded Monterey Jack cheese and sharp cheddar cheese evenly over the chorizo and vegetable mixture in the skillet.

If using, arrange the thinly sliced jalapeño peppers on top of the cheese.

Transfer the skillet to the preheated oven and bake for 10-15 minutes, or until the cheese is melted and bubbly.

Remove the skillet from the oven and let it cool for a few minutes before serving.

Garnish the queso fundido with chopped fresh cilantro, if desired.

Serve the queso fundido with chorizo and bell peppers hot, straight from the skillet, as a dip for tortilla chips or as a topping for sliced avocado.

Enjoy the gooey, cheesy goodness of Queso Fundido with Chorizo and Bell Peppers!

This dish is perfect for parties or gatherings and is sure to be a hit with friends and family. Feel free to customize it by adding other ingredients like diced tomatoes, black beans, or corn, and adjust the level of spiciness to your liking.

Mexican Deviled Eggs with Guacamole

Ingredients:

- 6 large eggs
- 1 ripe avocado
- 1 tablespoon lime juice
- 1 tablespoon finely chopped red onion
- 1 tablespoon finely chopped fresh cilantro
- 1 small jalapeño pepper, seeded and finely chopped (optional, for heat)
- Salt and pepper to taste
- Paprika or chili powder, for garnish
- Optional toppings: diced tomato, crumbled queso fresco, chopped fresh cilantro

Instructions:

Place the eggs in a single layer in a saucepan and cover them with water. Bring the water to a boil over medium-high heat.

Once the water reaches a rolling boil, remove the saucepan from the heat, cover it with a lid, and let the eggs sit in the hot water for 10-12 minutes.

After 10-12 minutes, drain the hot water from the saucepan and immediately transfer the eggs to a bowl of ice water to cool for about 5 minutes.

Once the eggs are cool, carefully peel off the shells and slice each egg in half lengthwise. Remove the yolks and transfer them to a mixing bowl.

Mash the ripe avocado in the mixing bowl with the egg yolks until smooth.

Add the lime juice, finely chopped red onion, finely chopped cilantro, and chopped jalapeño pepper (if using) to the avocado and egg yolk mixture. Season with salt and pepper to taste, and mix until well combined.

Spoon the guacamole mixture into the hollowed-out egg whites, dividing it evenly among the egg halves.

Sprinkle paprika or chili powder over the filled deviled eggs for garnish.

Optional: Top each deviled egg with diced tomato, crumbled queso fresco, or chopped fresh cilantro for extra flavor and presentation.

Chill the Mexican deviled eggs with guacamole in the refrigerator for at least 30 minutes before serving to allow the flavors to meld together.

Serve the deviled eggs chilled as a tasty appetizer or snack.

Enjoy your delicious and flavorful Mexican Deviled Eggs with Guacamole!

These Mexican-inspired deviled eggs are sure to impress your guests with their unique twist on a classic dish. They're perfect for parties, potlucks, or any occasion where you want to add a little fiesta to your menu.

Cheese Crisps with Jalapeño and Cilantro

Ingredients:

- 1 cup shredded cheese (such as cheddar, Monterey Jack, or Mexican blend)
- 1 jalapeño pepper, thinly sliced (seeds removed for less heat, if desired)
- 2 tablespoons chopped fresh cilantro

Instructions:

Preheat your oven to 375°F (190°C). Line a baking sheet with parchment paper or a silicone baking mat.
Place small mounds of shredded cheese on the prepared baking sheet, leaving space between each mound for spreading.
Flatten each mound of cheese slightly with the back of a spoon or your fingers to form thin rounds.
Arrange a few slices of jalapeño pepper and a sprinkle of chopped cilantro on top of each cheese round.
Bake the cheese crisps in the preheated oven for 5-7 minutes, or until the edges are golden brown and the cheese is bubbly and crispy.
Remove the baking sheet from the oven and let the cheese crisps cool on the pan for a few minutes.
Use a spatula to carefully transfer the cheese crisps to a wire rack to cool completely and crisp up further.
Once cooled, serve the cheese crisps with jalapeño and cilantro as a tasty snack or appetizer.
Enjoy your crunchy and flavorful cheese crisps with jalapeño and cilantro!

These cheese crisps are best enjoyed fresh, but you can store any leftovers in an airtight container at room temperature for up to 2 days. Reheat them in the oven for a few minutes to recrisp before serving, if desired. Feel free to customize the recipe with your favorite cheese blend or additional toppings like chopped green onions or diced tomatoes for added flavor.

Mexican Stuffed Mushrooms with Cheese and Chorizo

Ingredients:

- 16 large white button mushrooms, stems removed and cleaned
- 1/2 lb (225g) Mexican chorizo, casing removed
- 1/2 cup shredded Monterey Jack cheese
- 1/4 cup shredded cheddar cheese
- 1/4 cup diced onion
- 1 clove garlic, minced
- 1 jalapeño pepper, seeded and diced
- 2 tablespoons chopped fresh cilantro
- Salt and pepper to taste
- Optional toppings: diced tomato, chopped green onions, sour cream, or salsa

Instructions:

Preheat your oven to 375°F (190°C). Line a baking sheet with parchment paper or foil.

Remove the stems from the mushrooms and clean the caps with a damp paper towel. Place the mushroom caps on the prepared baking sheet, hollow side up.

In a skillet over medium heat, cook the Mexican chorizo until browned and cooked through, breaking it apart with a spoon as it cooks. Remove any excess grease from the skillet.

Add the diced onion, minced garlic, and diced jalapeño pepper to the skillet with the cooked chorizo. Cook for 2-3 minutes, or until the vegetables are softened.

Remove the skillet from the heat and stir in the chopped fresh cilantro. Season the mixture with salt and pepper to taste.

Spoon the chorizo mixture into the hollowed-out mushroom caps, filling each cap generously.

Sprinkle shredded Monterey Jack cheese and shredded cheddar cheese over the top of each stuffed mushroom.

Bake the stuffed mushrooms in the preheated oven for 15-20 minutes, or until the cheese is melted and bubbly and the mushrooms are cooked through.

Remove the stuffed mushrooms from the oven and let them cool slightly before serving.

Garnish the Mexican stuffed mushrooms with chopped fresh cilantro and optional toppings such as diced tomato, chopped green onions, sour cream, or salsa.

Serve the stuffed mushrooms warm as a tasty appetizer or snack.

Enjoy your flavorful and cheesy Mexican Stuffed Mushrooms with Cheese and Chorizo!

These stuffed mushrooms are sure to be a hit at any gathering or party. They're packed with savory flavors and have a satisfying texture that's perfect for munching on. Feel free to adjust the level of spiciness by adding more or less jalapeño pepper, and customize the toppings to suit your taste preferences.

Desserts:

Mexican Chocolate Avocado Mousse

Ingredients:

- 2 ripe avocados
- 1/4 cup cocoa powder
- 1/4 cup maple syrup or honey (adjust to taste)
- 1 teaspoon vanilla extract
- 1/2 teaspoon ground cinnamon
- 1/4 teaspoon chili powder (optional, for a spicy kick)
- Pinch of salt
- 1/4 cup milk (or dairy-free alternative such as almond milk or coconut milk)
- Optional toppings: whipped cream, shaved chocolate, sliced strawberries, or chopped nuts

Instructions:

Cut the avocados in half and remove the pits. Scoop the avocado flesh into a blender or food processor.
Add the cocoa powder, maple syrup or honey, vanilla extract, ground cinnamon, chili powder (if using), and a pinch of salt to the blender.
Pour in the milk or dairy-free alternative.
Blend the mixture until smooth and creamy, scraping down the sides of the blender or food processor as needed to ensure everything is well combined.
Taste the mousse and adjust the sweetness or seasoning as needed, adding more maple syrup, honey, or spices to suit your taste preferences.
Once the mousse reaches your desired consistency and flavor, transfer it to serving bowls or glasses.
Chill the Mexican Chocolate Avocado Mousse in the refrigerator for at least 30 minutes to allow it to firm up slightly and chill.
Before serving, garnish the mousse with optional toppings such as whipped cream, shaved chocolate, sliced strawberries, or chopped nuts.
Serve the Mexican Chocolate Avocado Mousse chilled and enjoy its rich and creamy texture!

This dessert is a decadent treat that's perfect for satisfying your sweet tooth while also providing some nutritional benefits from the avocado. The combination of chocolate with hints of cinnamon and chili powder creates a delightful flavor profile that's sure to impress. Feel free to experiment with different toppings and spices to customize the mousse to your liking.

Keto Tres Leches Cake

Ingredients:

For the cake:

- 1 cup almond flour
- 1/4 cup coconut flour
- 1/4 cup unsweetened cocoa powder
- 1 teaspoon baking powder
- 1/2 teaspoon baking soda
- 1/4 teaspoon salt
- 1/2 cup unsalted butter, melted
- 1/2 cup granulated erythritol or monk fruit sweetener
- 4 large eggs
- 1 teaspoon vanilla extract
- 1/2 cup unsweetened almond milk

For the tres leches mixture:

- 1/2 cup unsweetened almond milk
- 1/2 cup coconut milk
- 1/2 cup heavy cream
- 1 teaspoon vanilla extract
- 1/4 cup granulated erythritol or monk fruit sweetener

For the topping:

- 1 cup heavy whipping cream
- 1 tablespoon powdered erythritol or monk fruit sweetener
- Unsweetened cocoa powder, for dusting (optional)

Instructions:

For the cake:

Preheat your oven to 350°F (175°C). Grease a 9x9 inch baking pan with butter or cooking spray.
In a large mixing bowl, whisk together the almond flour, coconut flour, cocoa powder, baking powder, baking soda, and salt.

In another bowl, beat together the melted butter and granulated sweetener until well combined. Add the eggs one at a time, beating well after each addition. Stir in the vanilla extract.

Gradually add the dry ingredients to the wet ingredients, alternating with the almond milk, and mix until smooth.

Pour the batter into the prepared baking pan and spread it out evenly.

Bake in the preheated oven for 20-25 minutes, or until a toothpick inserted into the center comes out clean.

Remove the cake from the oven and let it cool slightly in the pan.

For the tres leches mixture:

In a mixing bowl, whisk together the almond milk, coconut milk, heavy cream, vanilla extract, and granulated sweetener until well combined.

Once the cake has cooled slightly, use a fork to poke holes all over the surface of the cake.

Slowly pour the tres leches mixture over the warm cake, allowing it to soak in evenly.

Cover the cake and refrigerate for at least 2 hours, or overnight, to allow the flavors to meld and the cake to absorb the liquid.

For the topping:

Before serving, whip the heavy whipping cream and powdered sweetener together until stiff peaks form.

Spread the whipped cream over the top of the chilled cake.

Optionally, dust the cake with unsweetened cocoa powder for decoration.

Slice and serve the keto tres leches cake chilled. Enjoy!

This keto-friendly version of Tres Leches Cake captures the essence of the traditional dessert while keeping the carbohydrate content low. Adjust the sweetness level according to your taste preferences, and feel free to customize the toppings with sliced strawberries or shaved chocolate.

Coconut Flan

Ingredients:

For the caramel:

- 1/2 cup granulated sugar
- 2 tablespoons water

For the flan:

- 4 large eggs
- 1 can (14 ounces) sweetened condensed milk
- 1 can (13.5 ounces) coconut milk
- 1 teaspoon vanilla extract
- 1/2 cup shredded coconut (optional, for added texture)

Instructions:

Step 1: Prepare the caramel

In a small saucepan, combine the granulated sugar and water over medium heat. Stir until the sugar is dissolved, then let it cook without stirring until it turns into a golden caramel, about 5-7 minutes. Swirl the pan occasionally to ensure even caramelization. Once the caramel reaches the desired color, immediately pour it into a round baking dish or individual ramekins, swirling to coat the bottom evenly. Be careful as the caramel will be very hot. Set aside to cool and harden.

Step 2: Prepare the flan mixture

Preheat your oven to 350°F (175°C).
In a large mixing bowl, whisk together the eggs, sweetened condensed milk, coconut milk, and vanilla extract until smooth and well combined. Stir in the shredded coconut if using.
Pour the flan mixture over the hardened caramel in the baking dish or ramekins.

Step 3: Bake the flan

Place the baking dish or ramekins in a larger baking pan. Pour hot water into the larger pan, being careful not to get any water into the flan mixture. The water should come about halfway up the sides of the baking dish or ramekins.
Carefully transfer the pan to the preheated oven and bake for 45-50 minutes, or until the flan is set but still jiggles slightly in the center.

Remove the flan from the oven and let it cool to room temperature. Then, cover and refrigerate for at least 4 hours or overnight to chill and set completely.

Step 4: Serve the flan

Once the flan is thoroughly chilled, run a knife around the edges of the baking dish or ramekins to loosen the flan.
Place a serving plate upside down over the top of the baking dish or ramekin and carefully invert to release the flan onto the plate. The caramel will flow over the top.
Slice and serve the coconut flan cold, garnished with additional shredded coconut if desired.

Enjoy the creamy and tropical flavors of homemade coconut flan! Adjust the sweetness according to your taste preferences, and feel free to experiment with different variations such as adding lime zest or rum extract for additional flavor.

Sugar-Free Churros with Cinnamon and Stevia

Ingredients:

For the churro dough:

- 1 cup water
- 1/2 cup unsalted butter
- 1 tablespoon granulated stevia or other sugar substitute
- 1/4 teaspoon salt
- 1 cup all-purpose flour
- 3 large eggs
- 1/2 teaspoon vanilla extract

For frying:

- Vegetable oil, for frying

For coating:

- 1/4 cup granulated stevia or other sugar substitute
- 1 teaspoon ground cinnamon

Instructions:

Step 1: Prepare the churro dough

In a medium saucepan, combine the water, butter, granulated stevia, and salt. Heat over medium heat until the mixture comes to a boil and the butter is melted.
Reduce the heat to low and add the flour all at once. Stir vigorously with a wooden spoon until the mixture forms a ball and pulls away from the sides of the pan, about 1-2 minutes.
Remove the saucepan from the heat and let the mixture cool for 5 minutes.
Once slightly cooled, add the eggs one at a time, stirring well after each addition, until the dough is smooth and glossy. Stir in the vanilla extract.

Step 2: Fry the churros

Heat vegetable oil in a deep skillet or saucepan to 375°F (190°C).
Transfer the churro dough to a piping bag fitted with a large star tip.
Pipe the dough directly into the hot oil, cutting it off with scissors or a knife to form 4-6 inch strips. Fry the churros in batches, being careful not to overcrowd the pan.

Fry the churros until golden brown and crispy, about 2-3 minutes per side. Use a slotted spoon or tongs to transfer them to a paper towel-lined plate to drain excess oil.

Step 3: Coat the churros

In a shallow dish, combine the granulated stevia and ground cinnamon.
While the churros are still warm, roll them in the cinnamon-stevia mixture until evenly coated.

Step 4: Serve the churros

Serve the sugar-free churros warm, either plain or with a side of sugar-free chocolate sauce or whipped cream for dipping.
Enjoy your delicious and guilt-free sugar-free churros with cinnamon and stevia!

These sugar-free churros are perfect for anyone looking to indulge in a classic treat without the added sugar. Adjust the sweetness to your taste preferences by adding more or less stevia, and feel free to get creative with your coatings and dipping sauces.

Mexican Spiced Dark Chocolate Truffles

Ingredients:

- 8 ounces (about 225g) dark chocolate (at least 70% cocoa), chopped
- 1/2 cup heavy cream
- 1 teaspoon ground cinnamon
- 1/2 teaspoon ground chili powder (adjust to taste)
- 1/4 teaspoon ground nutmeg
- 1/4 teaspoon ground cloves
- Pinch of salt
- 1 teaspoon vanilla extract
- Cocoa powder, for rolling
- Optional toppings: chopped nuts, shredded coconut, or cocoa powder for coating

Instructions:

Place the chopped dark chocolate in a heatproof bowl.
In a small saucepan, heat the heavy cream over medium heat until it just begins to simmer. Remove from heat.
Pour the hot cream over the chopped chocolate and let it sit for 1-2 minutes to soften the chocolate.
Stir the chocolate and cream together until smooth and well combined.
Add the ground cinnamon, ground chili powder, ground nutmeg, ground cloves, salt, and vanilla extract to the chocolate mixture. Stir until the spices are evenly incorporated.
Cover the bowl with plastic wrap and refrigerate the chocolate mixture for 1-2 hours, or until firm enough to handle.
Once chilled, use a spoon or a small cookie scoop to portion out the chocolate mixture and roll it into balls using your hands. Work quickly as the mixture may soften at room temperature.
Roll the chocolate truffles in cocoa powder or your desired coating until evenly coated. You can also roll them in chopped nuts, shredded coconut, or additional cocoa powder for extra flavor and texture.
Place the coated truffles on a baking sheet lined with parchment paper and refrigerate for another 30 minutes to firm up.
Once firm, transfer the truffles to an airtight container and store them in the refrigerator until ready to serve.
Serve the Mexican Spiced Dark Chocolate Truffles chilled and enjoy!

These truffles make a delightful treat for any occasion, and the combination of dark chocolate with warm Mexican spices adds a unique and delicious twist. Experiment with different coatings and toppings to customize the truffles to your taste preferences.

www.ingramcontent.com/pod-product-compliance
Lightning Source LLC
LaVergne TN
LVHW081604060526
838201LV00054B/2068